Revised Second Edition

# KEEN KUTTER

## An Illustrated Value Guide

By Jerry and Elaine Heuring

**COLLECTOR BOOKS**
P.O. Box 3009
Paducah, KY 42001

The current values in this book should be used only as a guide. They are not intended to set prices, which vary from one section of the country to another. Auction prices as well as dealer prices vary greatly and are affected by conditions as well as demand. Neither the authors nor the Publisher assumes responsibility for any losses that might be incurred as a result of consulting this guide.

Additional copies of this book may be ordered from:

COLLECTOR BOOKS
P.O. Box 3009
Paducah, Kentucky  42001

@ $14.95 - add $2.00 for postage and handling.

Copyright: Jerry and Elaine Heuring, 1990

This book or any part thereof may not be reproduced
without the written consent of the Author and Publisher.

## ACKNOWLEDGEMENTS

Our love and thanks is extended to our lovely teenage daughter, Wendy, for her participation in making this value guide. At fourteen, there were times when Wendy would have preferred to be "talking on the phone" rather than highlighting names and emblems on tools so they would appear clearly in our photos. We also appreciate the interest Wendy shows in our collection. We are always proud to have her go with us in our search for Keen Kutter. In fact, it was Wendy who found our Keen Kutter sewing machine.

A special "thank you" goes to Frank Bagbey, Doug Adams and Joel House of West Side Camera Shop in Cape Girardeau, Missouri, for their expertise, advise, guidance, and above all, patience in the help they gave us in getting our film developed properly.

# DEDICATION

TO WENDY MICHELLE
OUR LOVELY TEENAGER

# TABLE OF CONTENTS

# INTRODUCTION

This is our second edition of the Keen Kutter Value Guide. It has been five years since our first edition which was based solely on our collection. This edition, again based solely on our private collection, contains many different items than before due to the fact that our collection has more than tripled in size since 1983.

We take pride in our collection and show this by having a place in our home for each Keen Kutter item to be displayed. The only Keen Kutter items hidden in our closets are duplications which become saleable or trade items. Sometimes our collection is too convenient. We find ourselves using our Keen Kutter tools rather than going to the basement where the modern work tools are kept.

Perhaps you wonder what it was that inspired us to start a Keen Kutter collection. In 1972, when we started our careers, we relocated. Being out of college and in a different town, we found ourselves with nothing to do on weekends. We started going to auctions. Soon we had that contagious antique fever we heard so much about. Eventually we had such a variety of antiques and collectibles that we started doing shows and flea markets. We were intrigued as to how people would search and buy for collection purposes. We were doing no more than buying and selling antiques. In 1976, while doing an antique show, we decided that perhaps we should start a collection. After all, we were now living back "home" and were in the process of building a new house. We were beginning to get bored with buying and selling antiques. That day we purchased, for resale purposes, a Keen Kutter hatchet. We were looking at it and were impressed with the design of the logo or emblem. We decided rather than put a price on the hatchet we would start a Keen Kutter collection. Soon flea markets and shows became interesting again as we now had something to search for and call our own. Today we are still searching, only now we are a lot choosier. We only have an eye for rare quality tools, mint items and advertising pieces.

As in any collection, the condition of any item is critical in determining its value. If the name or logo is battered or unreadable, the value will be considerably less than if it would be in very good to mint condition. For example, if you have a regular claw hammer with the logo in good condition, you would have a $25.00 hammer. But, if that logo was scratched or unreadable, the hammer could be worth as low as $5.00. The items in our collection are in very good to mint condition. As any serious collector, we are always looking for the opportunity to upgrade any piece in our collection.

Our Keen Kutter collection has given us many hours of enjoyment. Through it we have made many contacts, many of which have become good friends. We look forward to sharing our stories about our finds with our fellow collectors and always enjoy hearing their stories in return. No matter how small or how big one's collection is, each piece holds a memory.

Although this value guide is primarily intended as a price guide, it is our hope that it will provide you with some helpful information and perhaps in addition a little humorous reminising of what perhaps you paid for a Keen Kutter piece years ago to use is valued at today.

Our wish for you – "HAPPY HUNTING."

# HISTORY

**Augustus Frederick Shapleigh 1810-1902**
**Edward Campbell Simmons 1839-1921**

Edward Campbell Simmons established the Simmons Hardware Company which was one of the most extensive corporations of its kind in the West.  E.C. Simmons was a prominent member of the hardware trade in St. Louis.  He was born in Frederick County, Maryland on September 21, 1839.  In 1846, when he was seven years of age, his father moved from Maryland, where he was a merchant, to St. Louis, Missouri. In 1856, being seventeen, E.C. Simmons entered the wholesale hardware establishment of Child, Pratt & Company in a minor capacity, at a salary of $12.50 per month.  After remaining with the firm for three years, he obtained a position as clerk with Wilson, Leavering & Waters in 1859, at a salary of $50.00 per month.  In 1862, three years later, he was admitted to the firm as a junior partner.  At the end of six months, Mr. Leavering died and the name of the firm was changed to Waters, Simmons & Company.  In 1866, E.C. Simmons married Carrie Welsh.  In 1870, the Simmons firm chose Keen Kutter as the brand for the line of high grade tools and cutlery.  Waters, Simmons & Company continued thus through nine years of great prosperity.  Mr. Waters retired January 1, 1872 and E.C. Simmons, associated with J.W. Morton and the firm became E.C. Simmons & Company.  Two years later in 1874, a corporation was formed under the name and style of the Simmons Hardware Company, which purchased the interests of E.C. Simmons & Company.  E.C. Simmons retired in 1898.

Augustus Frederick Shapleigh was born January 9, 1810 in Portsmouth, New Hampshire.  At the age of fourteen, he was employed at a hardware store in Portsmouth.  He worked there for one year, from daylight to dark, for $50.00 a year.  A.F. Shapleigh left the hardware store for a three-year period to lead a sailor's life and then returned.  Soon after returning, he was offered and accepted an important clerkship job with Rogers Brothers & Company, a wholesale hardware dealer in Philadelphia.  He worked for them for many years and obtained a junior partnership.  In 1843, A.F. Shapleigh was sent to the west to open a branch establishment of which he would serve as superintendent.  St. Louis, Missouri was the chosen location.  The firm called itself Rogers, Shapleigh & Company.  When Mr. Rogers died, A.F. Shapleigh formed a connection with Thomas D. Day, under the firm name of Shapleigh, Day & Company.  This firm existed sixteen years. Upon Mr. Day's retirement in 1863, the company became A.F. Shapleigh & Company. In 1864, the A.F. Shapleigh & Company adapted DIAMOND EDGE as the brand name for a line of superior tools and cutlery. A.F. Shapleigh retired in 1901.

Shapleigh's first catalog was issued in 1853 being a small paperback with no illustrations. By 1880 both Simmons Hardware Company and A.F. Shapleigh & Company published large, well bound general line catalogs. These catalogs, with the sole exception of one issued by Markley, Alling & Company of Chicago, were the first of their type to make an appearance in the hardware trade of the U.S.

Prosperous years followed for both Simmons Hardware Company and A.F. Shapleigh & Company. Their trade areas steadily expanded and eventually the combined sales of the two companies attained so large a volume as to firmly establish St. Louis as the largest distributor of hardware in the nation. Both E.C. Simmons and A.F. Shapleigh had the satisfaction of seeing their businesses carried on with constantly increasing strength and influence even after they themselves retired.

As a result of negotiations in the spring of 1940, Shapleigh Hardware Company purchased, for cash, all assets of Simmons Hardware Company effective July 1, 1940. Proceeds of the sale were distributed to stockholders of the Simmons Hardware Company whose charter was surrendered in due time. Upon purchase, Shapleigh Hardware Company occupied all of the buildings used by Simmons Hardware Company at Ninth and Spruce Streets as well as additional warehouse facilities on Poplar, Seventh to Eighth Streets in St. Louis.

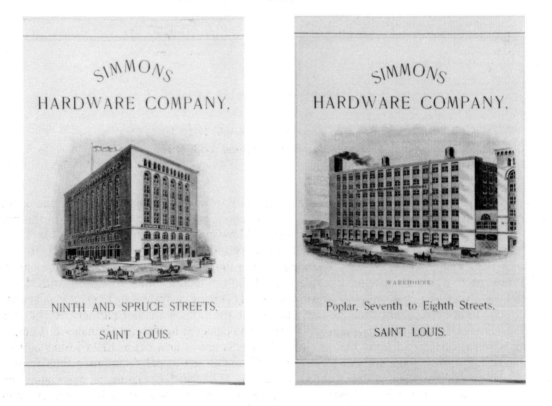

A majority of the Simmons Hardware Company personnel became associated with Shapleigh Hardware Company. All Simmons Hardware Company trademarked lines were continued and the business, thus greatly enlarged, operated smoothly and successfully under Shapleigh's management until its closing in the early 1960's.

# THE TRADEMARK

Every Keen Kutter tool was tested and inspected before being stamped with the trademark. The name and trademark was the maker's promise of superior quality. It was your protection as it guaranteed perfection or money refunded.

This is the trademark (logo/emblem). This emblem is off of a store display case, it is brass. Value $15.00.

The Keen Kutter trademark was adapted by Simmons Hardware Company in 1870. It was first applied to high grade axes. The favor with which they were received by the trade encouraged the immediate development of an extensive line of Keen Kutter tools and cutlery. The long standing Keen Kutter guarantee was: "We guarantee this tool to be properly made and tempered, and that the steel is free from manufacturing defects. If found otherwise and returned to us, we will give a new one for it."

The Keen Kutter slogan was: "The Recollection Of Quality Remains Long After The Price Is Forgotten." Sometimes this was wrote as "T R O Q R L A T P I F." The slogan was made famous by E.C. Simmons himself.

The Keen Kutter line was more than just so many tools. It was a complete line carefully planned and built to serve a very definite purpose. That purpose was to make easier the job of the retailer and user. E.C. Simmons said: "A jobber's first duty is to help his customer to prosper."

Throughout the Keen Kutter catalogs and want books you will find many phrases describing the product line. Here are a few:

Keen Kutter – the correct tool for every job.

Tools that work. Tools that are reliable. Tools that are ready when you are. Tools that will do hard work on hard material. Such tools are Keen Kutter quality tools.

Keen Kutter – the hardware brand for every demand.

A cutting edge for a generation. In cuttery your ideal of yesterday in the nation's choice of today. There is no substitute for Keen Kutter.

Every customer since 1894 a satisfied customer.

When in doubt, don't guess, just buy a Keen Kutter.

Keen Kutter tools, the best that brains, money and skill can produce.

They are the finest tools for the finest work. The most accurate tools for the most accurate workman. Keen Kutter quality tools are all the very highest quality, finest tools that can be made.

The better the tool, the better the work. There is one sure way to get the best tool for any purpose, ask for Keen Kutter quality tools.

Keen Kutter tools are made for hard work. Hard work doesn't hurt good tools, and tools to be good must do hard work.

Who were Keen Kutter products made for?

For the farmers, lawyers, doctors and merchants engrossed in the cares of their profession or business, yet frequently love to play at making things and to create with their hands.

For the skilled machanic, who, because of his expert knowledge, knows what is good when he sees it.

For the boy who loves tools, good tools, pretty tools.

# TOOL BOXES

Oak Wall Tool Cabinet

Dimensions are 27½" H, 19" W, and 8" Deep.  Value $225.00 - $250.00 with original decals (without tools).

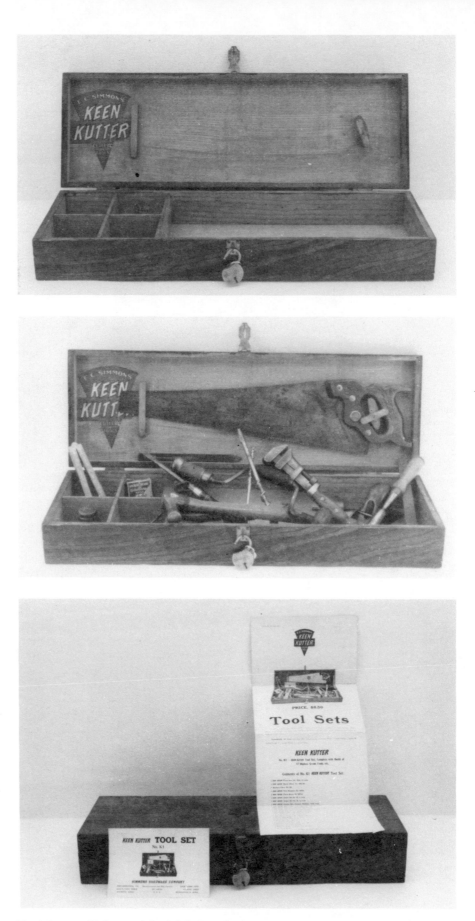

Tool box, still has original label and paperwork showing the contents. The size is 27½" x 9" x 5". Three photos showing empty, filled and closed with paperwork that came with it. Value of this box (without tools) $250.00 - $275.00.

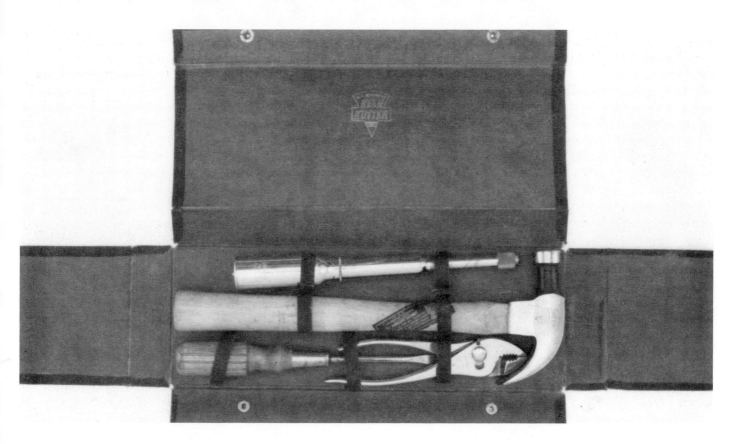

Tool Gift Set, includes hammer, screw driver, etc. in a black case, $300.00 - $325.00.

Leather Tool Box, logo stamped in leather below latch on outside. This condition, $150.00. If it had original decals on the inside and in good condition, the value would be $300.00.

# PLANES

**K64 Adjustable Iron Plane:** Combination, beading, rabbet and slitting combined. Nickel plated cast iron frame. Varnished Rosewood handles. Twenty-one highest grade crucible steel cutters in a brown canvas roll. Screw driver furnished, $450.00. ($600.00 in original box)

**KK115** Circular Plane, will cut concave or convex. $175.00 - $225.00.

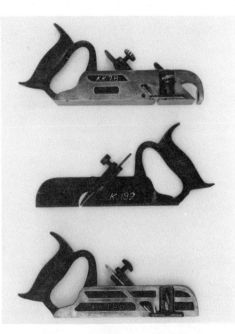

**Rabbet Planes: KK78,** rabbet and fillet-ster; **K192** 8" with 1" cutter; **K190** 8" with 1½" cutter. $85.00 - $115.00 each.

Plane, **KK212** Scraper and chamfer $100.00 - $125.00
Plane, **K76** Tongue and Groove, swing fence,
$85.00 - $115.00.

Router **K171,** patented 10-29-01. $100.00 - $125.00.

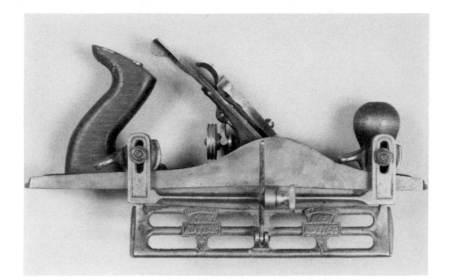

K5 Jack Plane with Fence: Smooth bottom with jointer or plane gauge attachment. Adjustable angles between 30° and 90°.
Plane, $40.00 - $45.00.   Attachment, $80.00 - $90.00.

Plane, KK10 carriage maker's rabbet, $150.00 - $175.00.
Plane, K240 scrub plane, 9½", $65.00 - $85.00.

Plane, KK4½ smooth iron plane, 10" - 2⅜" cutter, $50.00 - $75.00

Plane, Iron Smooth Plane KKM4 in original box, $65.00 - $75.00.

Planes: Corrugated (C) and Smooth Bottoms:
K3C, K4C and K5C, $45.00 - $55.00 each.
K5½C, $50.00 - $75.00.
K3, K4 and K5 (smooth bottom), $35.00 - $45.00.
K5½ (smooth bottom), $45.00 - $70-00.
These planes are marked on the ends and the blade is marked. The plane pictured upside down shows what a corrugated bottom looks like.

Iron Planes:
K6 fore, smooth bottom, $50.00 - $65.00.
KK7 jointer, corrugated bottom,
$60.00 - $75.00.
K8 jointer, smooth bottom,
$60.00 - $75.00.

Left:   K3   8" smooth iron, smooth bottom, $45.00 - $55.00.
Middle: K5   14" smooth iron, smooth bottom, $45.00 - $55.00.
Right:  K4   9" smooth iron, smooth bottom, $45.00 - $55.00.
Logos on these planes are on the lever cap.

16

Top: Iron Block Plane, K9½ in original box 6", $65.00 - $75.00.

Left: Iron Plane, KK4 Keen Kutter written on lever cap,
$40.00 - $45.00.
Iron Plane, KK6 Keen Kutter written on lever cap,
$45.00 - $65.00.

**Iron Block Planes:**
1st: KK9½ adjustable 6", $30.00 - $40.00.
2nd: KK15 7", $30.00 - $40.00.
3rd: KK18 knuckle joint adjustable 6", $35.00 - $45.00.
4th: KK60 low angle 6" with marking on the back, $30.00 - $40.00.
5th: K140 adjustable with removable side fence, $125.00 - $150.00.
    It can easily change from a block plane to a rabbet plane or vice versa. The right side is detachable.

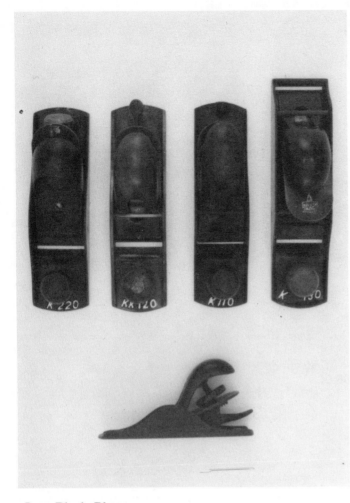

Iron Block Planes:
K220, adjustable, 7½" with old style cap, $20.00 - $30.00.
KK120, lever adjustment, 7½", $20.00 - $30.00.
K110, non-adjustable 7½", $20.00 - $30.00.
K130, double end, reversible (one for block plane and one for bullnose) not adjustable, 8", $40.00 - $50.00.
KK103, with lever adjustment 5½", $20.00 - $30.00.

Wooden Planes with old sawtooth markings. Sizes 10", 15" and 20". This was probably Keen Kutter's first logo. It is half-moon shaped with saw teeth design. These logos are found on the front wood base part of the plane as well as on the blade. $35.00 - $50.00 each.

Bull Nose Rabbet Plane, K75, not adjustable 4", $100.00 - $125.00.

Fore Planes, E.C. Simmons, all wooden: Top: 30", $50.00 - $75.00; Middle: 26", $45.00 - $55.00; Bottom: 15", $30.00 - $45.00.

18

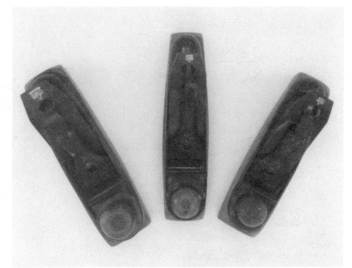

Top: K26 Wood Bottom Plane 15" length, 2⅛" cutter, $30.00 - $45.00;
Middle: K28 Wood Bottom Plane 18" length, $30.00 - $45.00;
Bottom: K31 Wood Bottom Plane 24" length, $45.00 - $55.00.

Planes, Smooth, wood bottom, adjustable: K24 9" length with 2" blade; K23 9" length with 1¾" blade; and K22 8" length with 1¾" blade, $30.00 - $40.00 each.

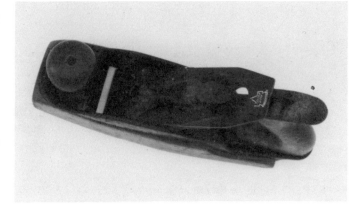

Plane, K35 handled smooth, wood bottom, 9", $40.00 - $45.00.

Replacement handle for plane, $8.00 - $12.00.

Top: K23 Plane 9" smooth wood bottom adjustable, $30.00 - $40.00.
Bottom: 8" coffin-shaped plane, $30.00 - $45.00. (Most markings are on the front, but occasionally they are on the side as in these two.)

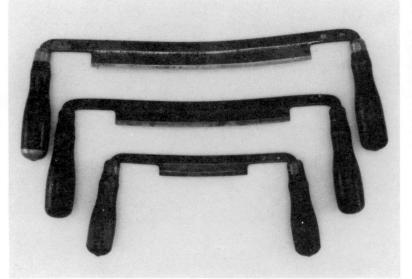

K10 Draw Knife with 10" blade, $15.00 - $20.00.
K8 Draw Knife with 8" blade, $15.00 - $20.00.
K4 Draw Knife with 4" blade, $35.00 - $45.00.

**Spoke Shaves:**
1st: KK96 cast iron frame, straight and concave
 cutters, $60.00 - $70.00.
2nd: KK92 cast iron frame, straight cutter,
 $50.00 - $60.00.
3rd: K95 concave cutter, $50.00 - $60.00.
4th: K91, $50.00 - $60.00.
5th: Wooden, varnished beechwood, straight
 cutter, $60.00 - $70.00.

Draw Knife, KLP 8" blade with offset handles, $45.00 - $55.00.

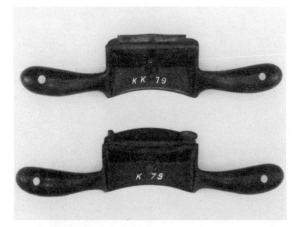

Cabinet Scraper Planes: KK79 and K79,
$50.00 - $60.00 each.

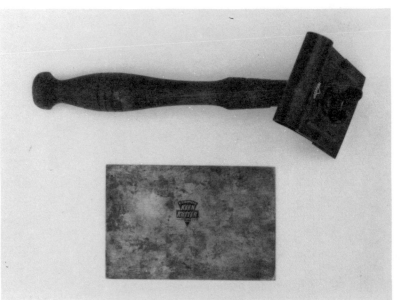

Scraper, floor and cabinet, $20.00 - $25.00.
Scraper, flat steel cabinet, $20.00 - $25.00.

# LEVELS, SQUARES AND RULES

Cast Iron Level 9" K69, $75.00 - $100.00.
Cast Iron Level 12" K612, $125.00 - $175.00.
Cast Iron Level 18" K618 adjustable,
$125.00 - $175.00.
Cast Iron Level 24" K624, $150.00 - $200.00.

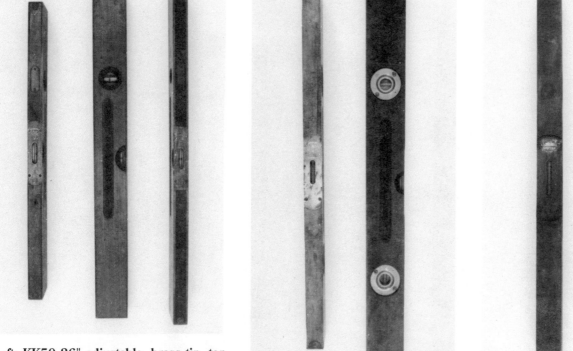

Masonary Level KK25, adjustable, brass button with logo on side, $65.00 - $95.00.

Left: KK50 26" adjustable, brass tip, top plate, brass bound, $75.00 - $125.00.

Middle: KK50 30" adjustable, brass tip, top plate, brass bound, $75.00 - $125.00.

Right: KK40 30" adjustable, brass tip, top plate, brass bound, has double duplex plates, $75.00 - $125.00.

Levels, adjustable, brass tip, top plate and double duplex plates: KK30 26" and KK30 30", $55.00 - $65.00 each.

Levels, non-adjustable, brass top plate: KK104 12" and 18", $40.00 - $45.00 each.

Levels, non-adjustable, brass top plate: KK13 12", 16" and 18", $40.00 - $45.00 each.

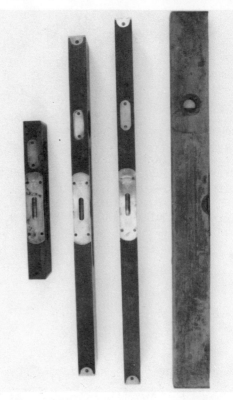

Levels, adjustable, cast-brass tips and top plate:
12"   KK3,   $45.00 - $65.00.
26"   KK3,   $30.00 - $40.00.
28"   KK3,   $30.00 - $40.00.
30"   KK3,   $30.00 - $40.00.

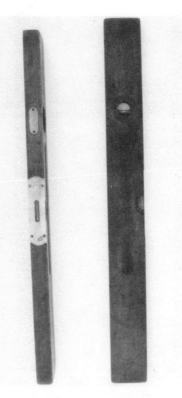

Levels, adjustable, brass top plate:
28"   KK2,   $25.00 - $30.00.
30"   KK2 square name plate,
         $25.00 - $30.00.

Levels, non-adjustable, brass top.
#KK0 sizes 24", 26", 28" and 30",
$25.00 - $30.00 each.

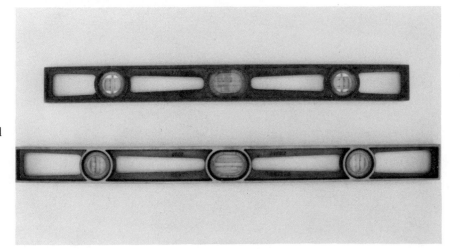

Levels, Shapleigh cast aluminum 24" and
28", $30.00 - $35.00 each.

Levels, Shapleigh, non-adjustable:
12"  F3-753GK,  $30.00 - $45.00.
24"  F3-754GK,  $30.00 - $45.00.
28"  F3-755GK,  $30.00 - $45.00.

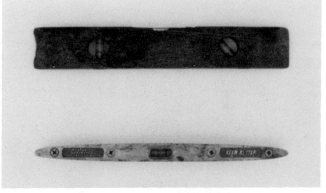

Pocket or Torpedo Levels, F3764GK wood and a cast
aluminum level, $30.00 - $35.00 each.

Take Down Square, $150.00 - $175.00.

23

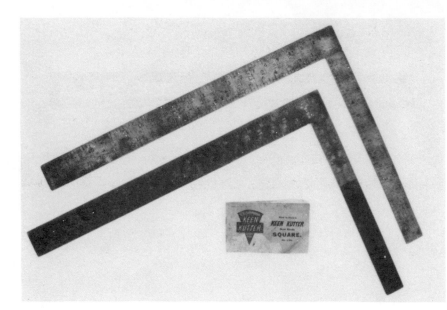

Top: Square, K3 Blue Brand,
   $18.00 - $25.00.
Middle: Square, KC3 copper finish,
   $18.00 - $25.00.
Bottom: Square, K100 book on "How To
   Use A Keen Kutter Square,"
   $25.00 - $35.00.

Square, K18, 12" long tongue,
$25.00 - $35.00.
Square, K10, 8" long tongue,
$35.00 - $45.00.
K312, 12" long steel rule,
$25.00 - $35.00.

1st: Tri Square, 10" blade, cast iron handle,
   $25.00 - $30.00.
2nd: Tri Square, 6" blade, cast iron handle,
   $25.00 - $30.00.
3rd: Tri and Mitre, 6" blade, cast iron handle,
   $25.00 - $30.00.
4th: Combination Square, $35.00 - $45.00.

Left: 7½" tri and mitre square, wooden handle,
   logo on blade, $20.00 - $25.00.
Middle: 6" tri & mitre square, wooden handle,
   logo on blade, $20.00 - $25.00.
Right: 4½" tri square, wooden handle, logo on
   blade, $20.00 - $25.00.

24

Sliding T-Bevel Squares with cast iron handles, 8" blade and 10" blade, $35.00 - $45.00 each.

Sliding T-Bevel Squares, wood handles, logo on blades:
1st:   6" blade, $35.00 - $45.00.
2nd:  8" blade, $35.00 - $45.00.
3rd:  10" blade, $30.00 - $40.00.

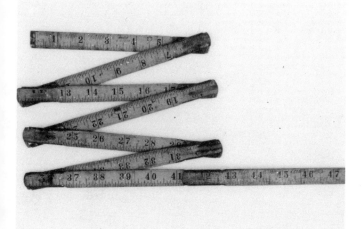

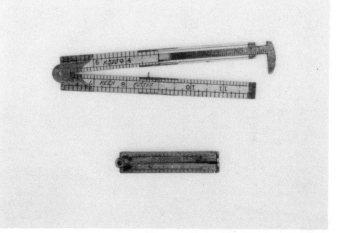

K504 4' 8-fold rule enameled yellow patented June 5, 1900, $75.00 - $100.00.

Top: Boxwood Rule, K320 caliper, 1' four-fold, 1" wide folded (mint), $75.00 - $85.00.
Bottom: Boxwood Rule, K690, 1' four-fold unbound, ⅝" wide folded, $20.00 - $30.00.

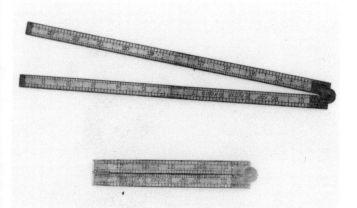

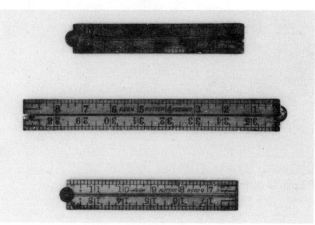

Top: Folding Rule, K840 2' four-fold half-bound, 1" wide folded, Boxwood, $30.00 - $45.00.
Bottom: K620 2' four-fold full-bound, 1" wide folded, Boxwood, $30.00 - $45.00.

Top: K610 2' four-fold unbound 1" wide folded, $20.00 - $35.00.
Middle: K660½ 3' four-fold unbound 1" wide folded, $25.00 - $40.00.
Bottom: K680 2' four-fold unbound 1" wide folded, $20.00 - $35.00.

Top: Junior Steel Tape Measure, E.C. Simmons, 100' steel with Keen Kutter written on tape #K82, $70.00 - $90.00.
Middle: Tape Measure F5006GK, give-away made by Lufkin and has Lufkin tape in it, $15.00 - $20.00.
Bottom: Tape Measure, E.C. Simmons K73 with E.C. Simmons wrote on the tape, $50.00 - $60.00.

# SAWS

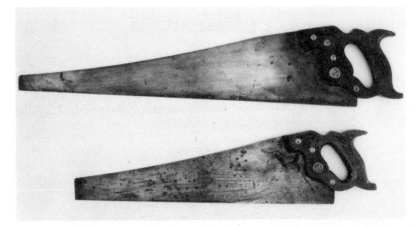

Handsaws (to show size comparison)

Top: K88, 26", $45.00 - $55.00.
Bottom: K88S, 20" for use in tool box kits, $45.00 - $55.00.

Handsaws, K18 and K726S, 26".
If logo is still on blade, $45.00 - $55.00.

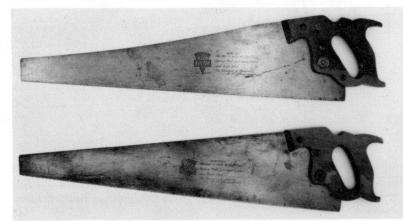

Handsaws: K24 and K88S with 26" blade cut, logo still written on the blade, $45.00 - $55.00 each.

Top: K88 20" saw, $45.00 - $55.00.
Bottom: Saw with 20" blade with original marking Keen Kutter written out, button has Keen Kutter with axe head on it, $45.00 - $55.00. If the saw is rough and worn and only has the button, the price could start as low as $5.00.

Top: Flooring saw, adjustable, $65.00.
Bottom: K44 Back Saw, $45.00 - $55.00.

Stair Builder's Saw, KK6, highest grade crucible steel blade, applewood handle. Mint condition, $60.00 - $70.00.

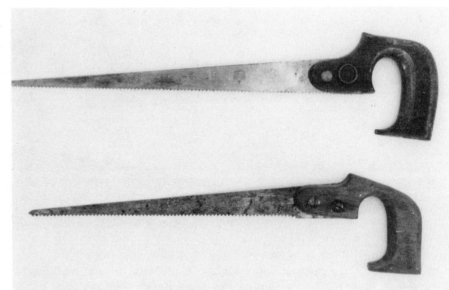

Top: Compass Saw, Shapleigh 14" blade, $15.00 - $20.00.
Bottom: Keyhole Saw, E.C. Simmons, 10" blade, $15.00 - $20.00.

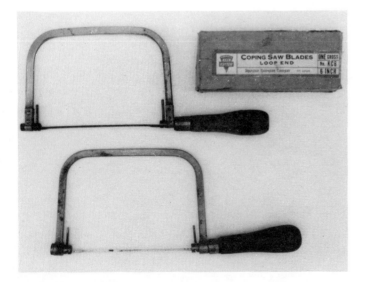

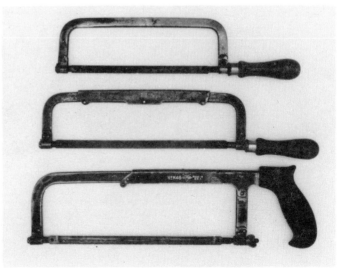

Coping Saw, K50 heavy pattern with logo; Coping saw with Keen Kutter written out, $15.00 - $20.00 each.
Coping Saw Blade in original box, $20.00 - $25.00.

Hack Saws K188, not adjustable; K188A adjustable and K48 adjustable, $35.00 - $45.00 each.

Metal Cutting Saw, Shapleigh #K106, 15 teeth per inch, still has label on it, $75.00 - $85.00.

#K Saw Tool for one or two man cross cut saw with setting block (top item), $20.00 - $25.00.

Saw setting hammer, 7 oz. with original sticker (never used, mint), $35.00 - $45.00; Used, normal wear, $20.00 - $25.00.

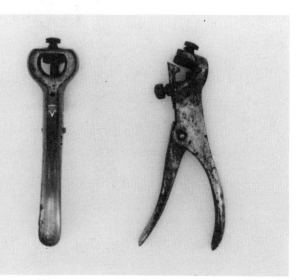

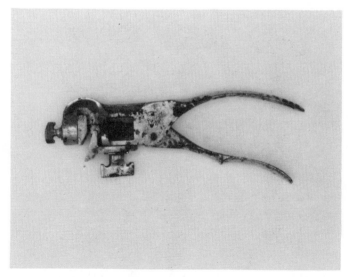

Saw Set, K10, $12.00 ⸲ $18.00.
Saw set with Keen Kutter written on inside of handle, $12.00 - $18.00.

Saw Set, wide tooth for cross cut saw, $15.00.

# HAMMERS

Hammers, E.C. Simmons, round neck, curved claw:
1st: 20 oz., $25.00 - $30.00.
2nd: 16 oz., $25.00 - $30.00.
3rd: 13 oz., $25.00 - $30.00.
4th: 7 oz., $55.00 - $65.00.

Hammers (left to right):
1st: Shapleigh 20 oz. with steel shank, straight claw, rubber handle, $20.00 - $25.00.
2nd: Shapleigh 16 oz. curved claw, hexagon neck, rubber handle, $20.00 - $25.00.
3rd: Shapleigh 16 oz. hexagon neck, wood handle, $20.00 - $25.00.
4th: Shapleigh 13 oz. hexagon neck, wood handle, $20.00 - $25.00.
5th: E.C. Simmons 7 oz. hexagon neck, curved claw, $55.00 - $65.00.

Hammers: E.C. Simmons, Ball Pein sizes 24 oz., 20 oz., 16 oz. $35.00 - $40.00 each.

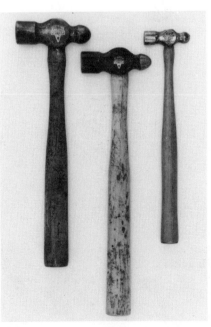

Hammers, Shapleigh Ball Pein sizes 6 oz., 8 oz., 12 oz. and 16 oz., $35.00 - $40.00 each.

Hammers:
Ball Pein sizes 8 oz. and 12 oz., $35.00 - $40.00 each.
Hammer, small Ball Pein, $55.00 - $65.00.

Top Two: Blacksmith shop Hammers,
$35.00 - $45.00 each.
3rd: Blacksmith-Riveters Flat Top
Hammer with hole in it,
$45.00 - $55.00.
4th: Straight Pein, $45.00 - $55.00.

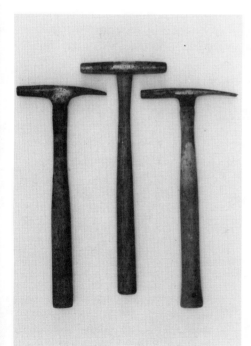

Hammers:
Left and middle are two different Tack
Hammers, $15.00 - $20.00 each.
Right: Upholstery Hammer,
$15.00- $20.00.

Bill Posters Hammers, 5 oz.
#K55 and 8 oz. #K85,
$20.00 - $25.00 each.

Tinner's Hammers, three different sizes.
$20.00 - $25.00.

Brick Hammers, head lengths of 8½", 7½" and 6½", $35.00 - $45.00 each.
Brick Hammer with 5½" head length, $45.00 - $55.00.

Left:  Shoe Cobbler Hammer, $35.00 - $45.00.
Right: Prospecting Pick, $35.00 - $45.00.

Mallets: Wooden mallets, the large one has a double Keen Kutter stamp on it. The other is a rubber mallet.  $30.00 - $40.00 each.

# CHISELS AND PUNCHES

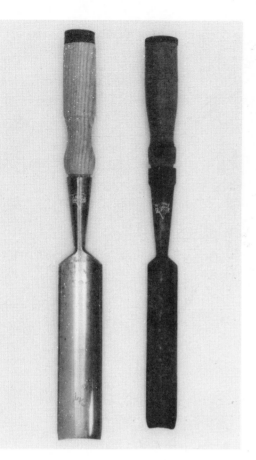

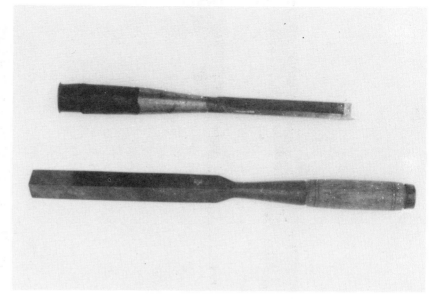

Socket Corner Chisels sizes ¾" and ⅞", $25.00 - $30.00 each.

Gouge 1" and 1½",  $30.00 - $35.00 each.

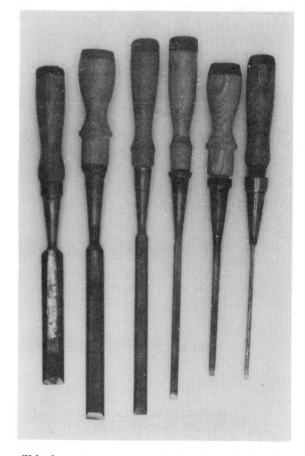

Chisels:
Sizes ⅜", ½" and 1", $10.00 - $12.00 each.
Sizes 1½" and 2", $12.00 - $15.00 each.

Chisels:
Sizes ⅛", 3/16" and ¼", $12.00 - $15.00 each.
Sizes ⅝", ¾" and ½", $10.00 - $12.00 each.

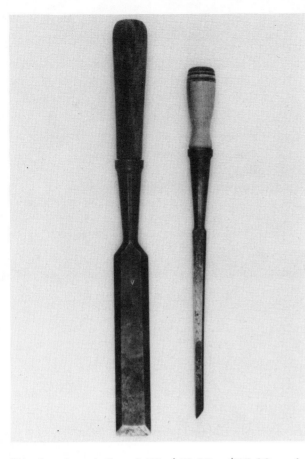

Chisels, sizes 1½" and ⅜", $12.00 - $15.00 each.

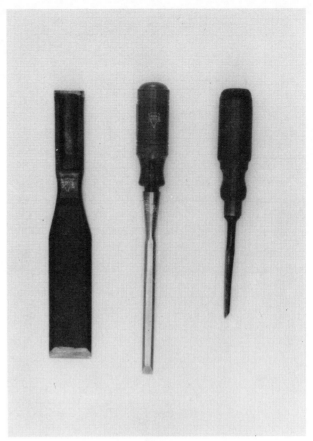

Left: Odd chisel, 1½" no handle,  $10.00.
Middle: Shapleigh ⅜" plastic handle,
        $10.00 - $12.00.
Right: Tanged-butt ¼", $15.00 - $18.00.

Cape Chisels, three different sizes,
$10.00 - $12.00 each.

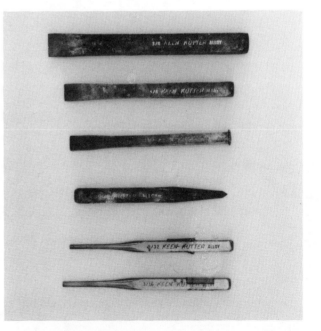

1st Three: Set of Cold Chisels sizes ¾", ⅝" and ½",
        $8.00 - $12.00 each.
4th: Center Punch, $8.00 - $12.00.
5th: ⁵⁄₃₂ Machinist Punch, $8.00 - $12.00.
6th: ³⁄₁₆ Machinist Punch, $8.00 - $12.00.

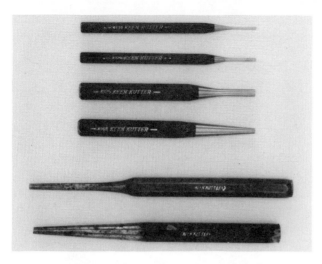

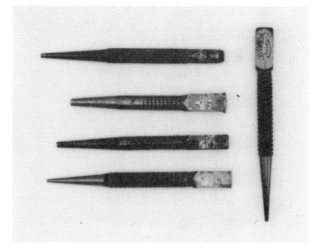

1st Four: Machinist Punches, $8.00 - $12.00 each.
5th: Pin Punch, $8.00 - $12.00.
6th: Machinist Drift, $8.00 - $12.00.

Nail Sets, five different types, $8.00 - $12.00 each.

# BRACES AND BITS

Tag for braces, $7.00 - $10.00.

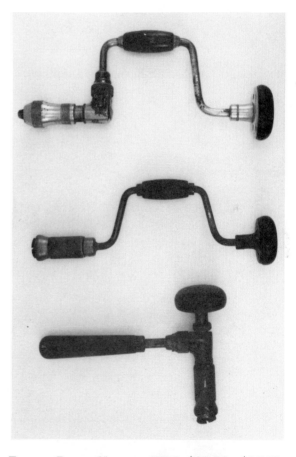

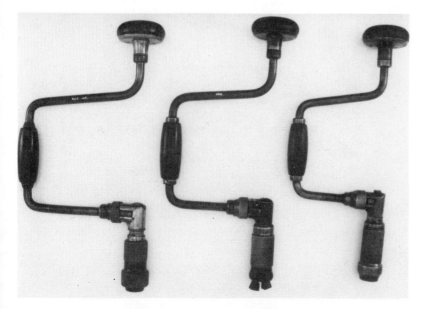

Top: Brace, 8" sweep #K18, $20.00 - $25.00.
Middle: Brace, 6" sweep #KA6, $20.00 - $25.00.
Bottom: Hand-held Ratchet Brace,
        $60.00 - $75.00.

Left: Brace #KBB 14", $20.00 - $25.00.
Middle: Brace #KB 13", $20.00 - $25.00.
Right: Brace #KB 12", $20.00 - $25.00.

Breast Drill, $40.00 - $60.00.

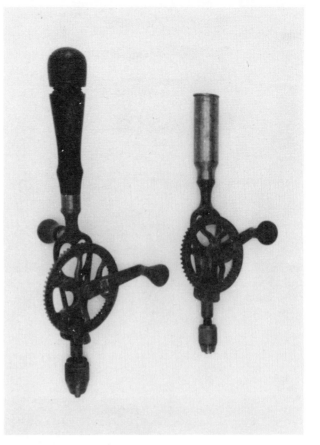

Hand Drill (small one) hollow brass handle, holds either fluted drill points or any twist drills, has revolving cap with separate index compartments for drill points, $50.00 - $60.00. Hand Drill (large one) handle has removable top to hold twist bits, $50.00 - $60.00.

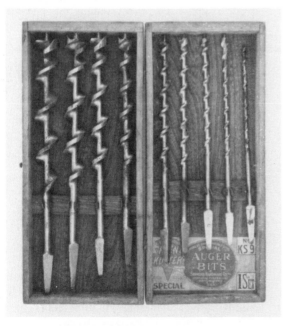

Auger Bits #KS9 in original box, $95.00 - $105.00.

Auger Bit Set of thirteen sizes from $4/16$ to $16/16$, $85.00 - $95.00.

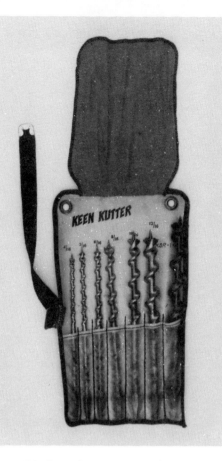

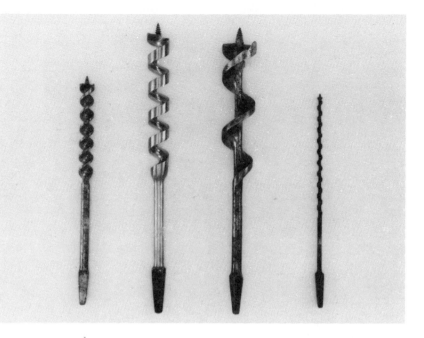

1st: Auger Bit, #8 on Jennings Pattern, $5.00 - $7.00.
2nd: #13 Ship Auger Bit $^{13}/_{16}$, $5.00 - $7.00.
3rd: Auger Bit 1¼", $8.00 - $10.00.
4th: Auger Bit $^{3}/_{16}$", $8.00 - $10.00.

Auger Bit Set of seven sizes from $^{4}/_{16}$ to $^{16}/_{16}$ in a roll up case, $65.00 - $75.00.

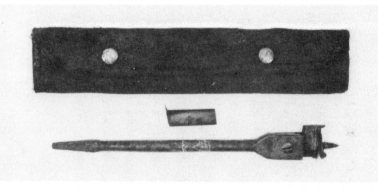

Expansion Bit with original canvas pouch which has brass Keen Kutter marked buttons, $30.00 - $35.00.

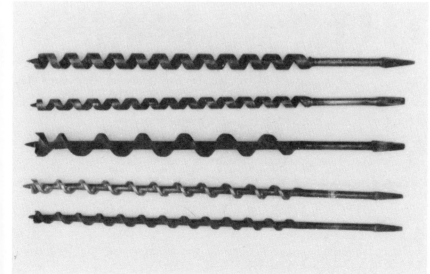

Top: #12 Ship Auger Car Bit ¾", $10.00 - $12.00.
2nd: #8 Ship Auger Car Bit ½", $10.00 - $12.00.
3rd: #17 Car Bits 1$^{1}/_{16}$" (rod thru look), $8.00 - $10.00.
4th: #11 Car Bits $^{11}/_{16}$" (rod thru look), $8.00 - $10.00.
5th: #9 Car Bits $^{9}/_{16}$" (rod thru look), $8.00 - $10.00.

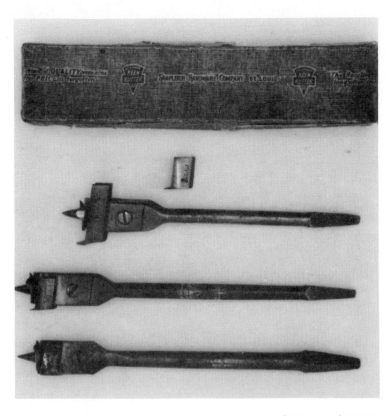

Expansion Bit F6028GK ⅞ to 3", original box, $20.00 - $25.00. Expansion Bit with logo, patent date 3-12-13 and one with Keen Kutter written out on it, $10.00 - $15.00 each.

Bit Stock Drills K-16 in container with 9 bits, $100.00 - $125.00.

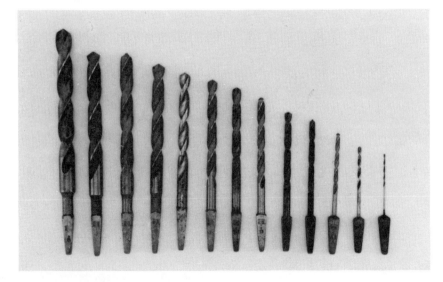

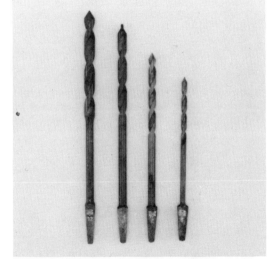

Bit Stock Drills for metal or wood sizes %₁₆, ½, ⁷⁄₁₆, ¹⁵⁄₃₂, ⅜, ¹¹⁄₃₂, ⁵⁄₁₆, **8**, ⁹⁄₃₂, **7**, ⅛, ⁵⁄₃₂, ¹⁄₁₆.  $3.00 - $5.00 each.

Electrician or Bell Hangers Bits sizes 12, 10, 8 and 6, $8.00 - $10.00 each.

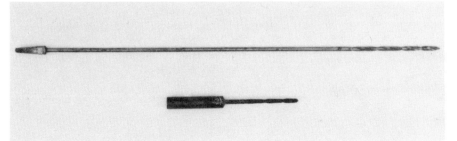

Bell Hanger Bit #6 (long one), $7.00 - $8.00.
Post Drill Bit ³⁄₁₆" (short one), $7.00 - $8.00.

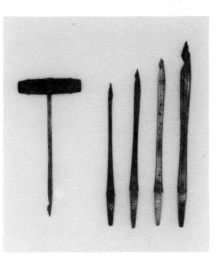

Gimlet with wood handle,
$8.00 - $10.00.
Gimlet bits to fit a brace,
four different sizes,
$5.00 - $6.00 each.

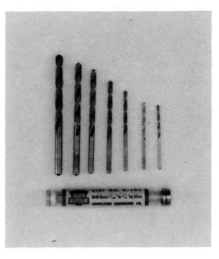

Twist Drill Set, 7 bits sizes 1/16 to 1/4
by 32nds and round tube container,
set $50.00 - $60.00.

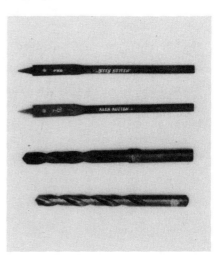

1st: Spade Bit 3/8" for wood,
$8.00 - $10.00.
2nd: Spade Bit 7/16" for wood,
$8.00 - $10.00.
3rd: Twist Drill Bit 7/16",
$8.00 - $10.00.
4th: Twist Drill Bit 13/32",
$8.00 - $10.00.

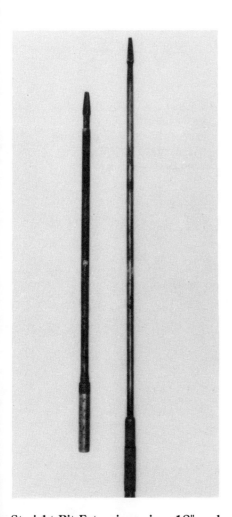

Straight Bit Extensions sizes 18" and
24", $20.00 - $25.00 each.

Screw Driver Bits, set of three,
$15.00 - $20.00 set.

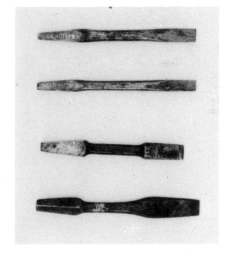

Screw Driver Bits, four different
types, $6.00 - $8.00 each.

Alligator Wrench, adjustable with patent date of 5-26-03, $100.00 - $125.00.

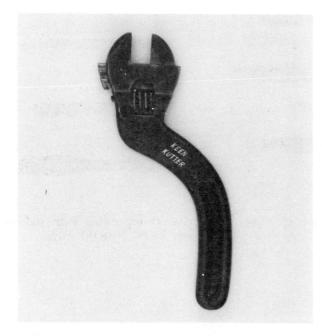

Left: K40 Alligator Wrench, combination bolt wrench, $50.00 - $65.00.

Middle: K23 Combination Bolt Wrench and Thread Cutter, $50.00 - $65.00.

Right: K15 Combination Bolt Wrench, $60.00 - $75.00.

Adjustable S Wrench with logo stamped in jaw and Keen Kutter written on handle, $85.00 - $100.00.

Left: K96 Automobile Wrench with pry on the end, $35.00 - $40.00.

Right: K95 Automobile Wrench, $35.00 - $40.00.

Screw Wrenches, wooden handles, logo on wrenches:
1st:  6"  $45.00 - $50.00.     5th: 15" $35.00 - $45.00.
2nd: 8"  $40.00 - $45.00.     6th: 18" $45.00 - $50.00.
3rd: 10" $35.00 - $45.00.     7th: 21" $60.00 - $65.00.
4th: 12" $35.00 - $45.00.

Pipe Wrenches with Keen Kutter wrote on handles:
1st:  8" $25.00 - $30.00.     4th: 14" $18.00 - $25.00.
2nd: 10" $20.00 - $25.00.     5th: 18" $18.00 - $25.00.
3rd: 12" $18.00 - $25.00.     6th: 24" $30.00 - $35.00.

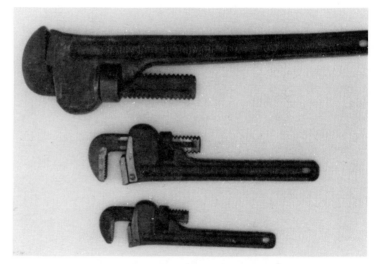

Wrenches, all steel with logo: 8", 10" and 12", $25.00 - $35.00 each.

Pipe Wrenches, Shapleigh 8", 10" and 18", $15.00 - $20.00 each.

Pipe Wrench, interchangeable jaw, $30.00 - $35.00.

Pipe Wrench, 8" with wood handle, $20.00 - $25.00.

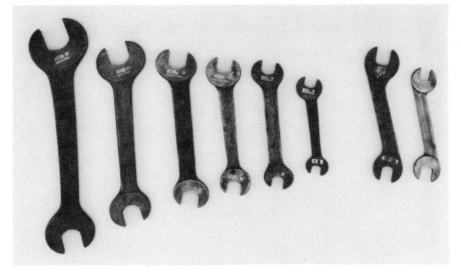

Wrenches, $20.00 - $25.00 each.
(left to right):

1st: K34   size ½ & ⅝ Engineer's wrench
2nd: K31  size ½ & ⁷⁄₁₆ Engineer's wrench
3rd: K29  size ⅜ & ⁷⁄₁₆ Engineer's wrench
4th: K727 size ⅜ & ⁷⁄₁₆ Cape screw wrench
5th: K25  size ¼ & ⁵⁄₁₆ Engineer's wrench
6th: K23  size ¼ & ³⁄₁₆ Engineer's wrench
7th: KT3  size ¼ & ⁵⁄₁₆ Textile and Machine wrench
8th: KT3  size ¼ & ³⁄₁₆ Textile and Machine wrench

General Purpose Wrenches, Keen Kutter is written on end, $20.00 - $25.00 each.

1st: K1000 ½ & ⁷⁄₁₆
2nd: K750 ⅜ & ⁷⁄₁₆
3rd: K580 ⅜ & ⁵⁄₁₆
4th: K500 ¼ USS & ⁵⁄₁₆ USS
5th: "S" wrench with emblem on top, no number on it.

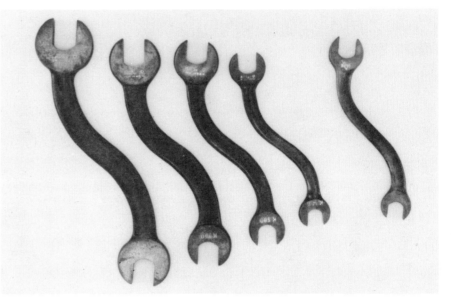

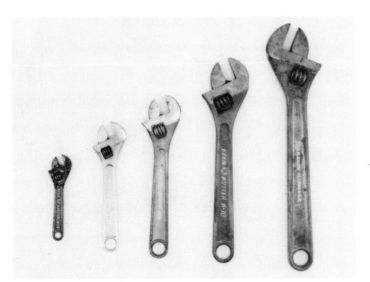

Adjustable Wrenches, Shapleigh Keen Kutter:
1st: K4,   $40.00 - $50.00.    4th: K10, $20.00 - $25.00.
2nd: K6,  $20.00 - $25.00.    5th: K12, $30.00 - $35.00.
3rd: K8,  $15.00 - $20.00.

Angle Adjustable Wrenches, E.C. Simmons:
Top: #10, $15.00 - $20.00.
Bottom: #6, $20.00 - $25.00.

# PLIERS

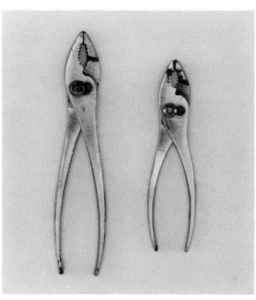

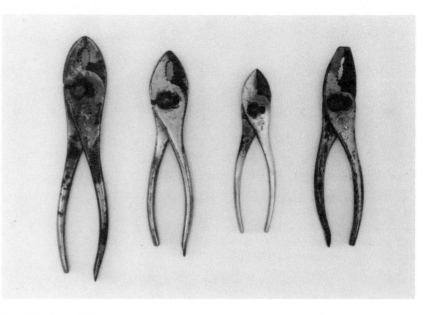

Left: Combination Pliers K180,
   $15.00 - $20.00.
Right: Combination Pliers K160,
   $15.00 - $20.00.

Combination Pliers:
1st: 8" with screwdriver on end of handle, $15.00 - $20.00.
2nd: 7" with screwdriver on end of handle, $15.00 - $20.00.
3rd: 5½" thin nose, $20.00 - $25.00.
4th: 6½" thin narrow 30° bent nose slip joint with screw driver on end
   of handle, $20.00 - $25.00.

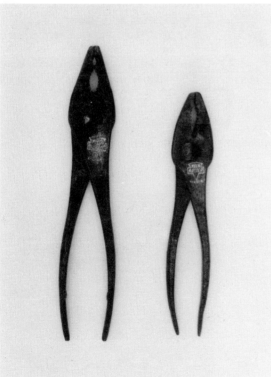

Combination Pliers K51-8 and K51-10,
$15.00 - $20.00 each.

Channel Lock Pliers, $20.00 - $25.00 each.
Left: K57
Right: K507 - 6½"
Bottom: K750 - 75° angle head combination
pliers and pipe wrench.

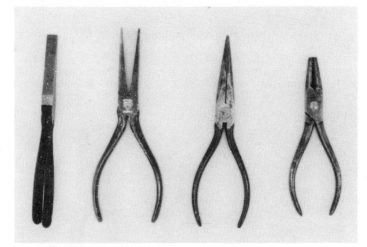

1st: Pliers, K86-6 (side view) ⅜" wide, flat nose, $30.00 - $35.00.
2nd: Pliers, ¼" flat nose, $30.00 - $35.00.
3rd: Pliers, K66-6 round or needle nose, $20.00 - $25.00.
4th: Pliers, round nose, $20.00 - $25.00.

Milliners or Radio Pliers, 5" long, has long curved nose, $35.00 - $40.00.

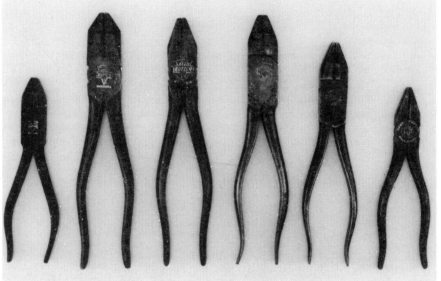

Side Cutters & Lineman Pliers, $20.00 - $25.00 each.

1st:  6" long with logo
2nd: 8½" long with logo
3rd:  8" long #K85-8 with logo
4th:  8" long with logo
5th:  7½" long #950 Keen Kutter written out
6th:  6" long - both logo and Keen Kutter written out

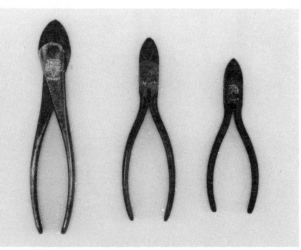

Diagonal Cutting Pliers:
Left: K47-7, $20.00 - $25.00.
Middle: K45-6, $20.00 - $25.00.
Right: K45-5, $20.00 - $25.00.

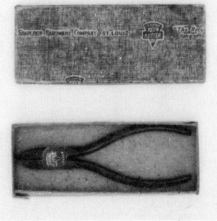

Pliers, K45-5 Diagonal in original box, $40.00 - $45.00.

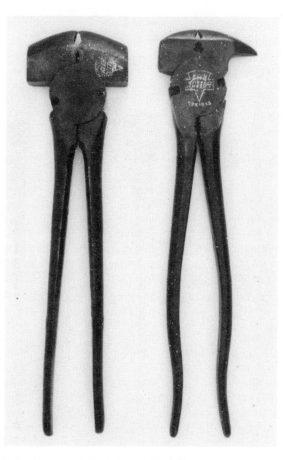

Pliers and Wire Cutter Combined, $25.00 - $30.00.
Left: KB10, 10" long.
Right: Keen Kutter written out on handle, patented Feb. 5, 1901, 4⅝" overall length.

Gas Pipe and Battery Pliers, 8" long and 10" long, $25.00 - $30.00.

Left: Staple Puller, head 2⅝" long, $20.00 - $25.00.
Right: Fence Plier and Staple Puller #K1946, head 2⅝" long, $20.00 - $25.00.

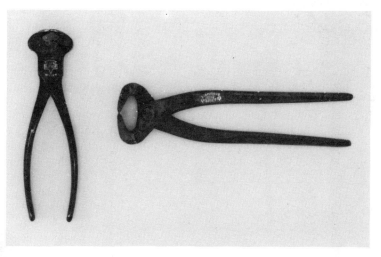

Carpenter Pinchers, two different types, $12.00 - $18.00 each.

Carpenter Pinchers, four different types, $12.00 - $18.00 each.

45

# SCREW DRIVERS

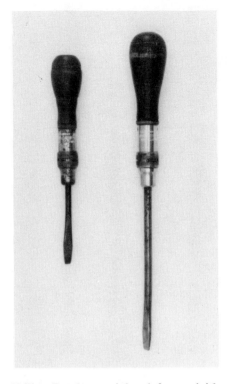

Utility Ratchets, right, left or rigid, $50.00 - $60.00 each.

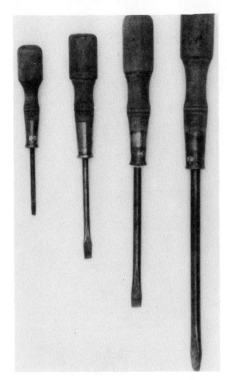

Screw Drivers with brass ferrules sizes 2½", 4", 6" and 8", $18.00 - $25.00 each.

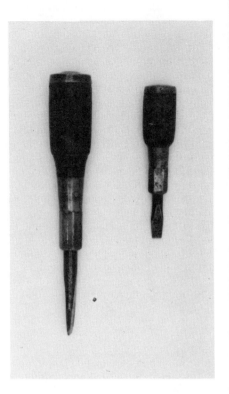

Machinists Screw Drivers, two different types, $15.00 - $20.00 each.

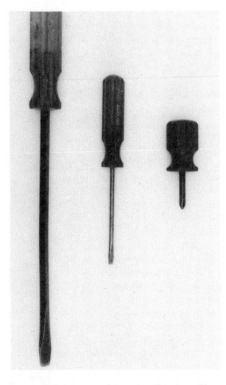

Screw Drivers with plastic handles: regular square shank with 10" blade, cabinet round shank, and a stubby Phillips type, $7.00 - $10.00 each.

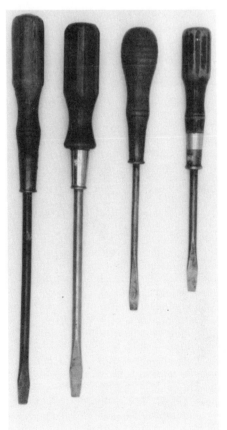

1st: Screw Driver K50 with 8" blade, $12.00 - $18.00.

2nd: Screw Driver K50 with 8" blade, different handle style, $12.00 - $18.00.

3rd: Screw Driver K615 with 6" blade, $12.00 - $18.00.

4th: Screw Driver K40 with 5" blade with brass ferrules, $18.00 - $25.00.

# FILES

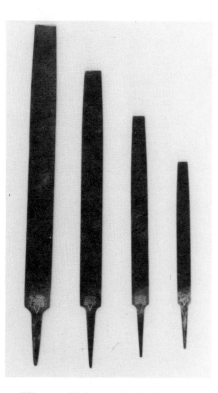

Files, mill bastard single cut,
$7.00 - $12.00 each.

Files, double cut mill bastard,
$7.00 - $12.00 each.

Files, half-round wood,
$7.00 - $12.00 each.

Rasps, half-round wood,
$7.00 - $12.00 each.

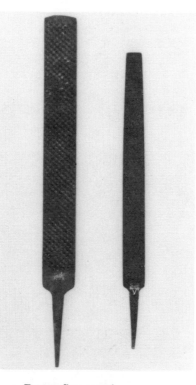

Rasp, flat wood,
$7.00 - $12.00 each.

Rasps, two plain slim horse rasps
(large ones), two half round shoe
rasps (small ones), $7.00 - $12.00
each.

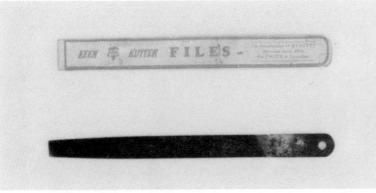

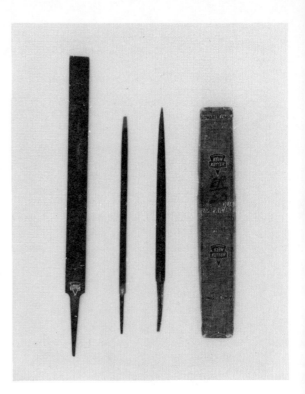

File box, $10.00.   File with hole in it, $7.00 - $12.00.

Left: Cant-saw file, $7.00 - $12.00.
Middle: Files, two KCSS6 slim taper,
$7.00 - $12.00 each.
Right: File box, $10.00.

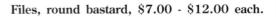

Files, round bastard, $7.00 - $12.00 each.

# TAP AND DIE SETS

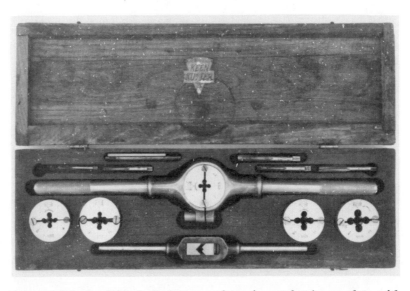

Tap and Die Set K31 (called screw plates in catalogs) complete with
five size taper tape dies and guides in original wooden box,
$250.00 - $300.00.

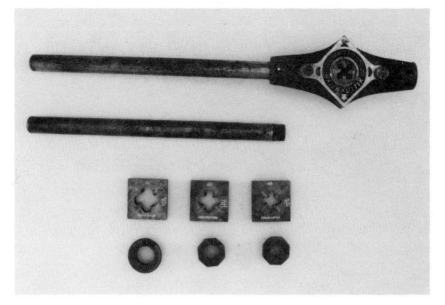

Tap and Die Set, small set in original wooden box, $200.00 - $250.00.

Pipe Stocks and Dies with four different size cutters ¼, ⅜, ½, ¾, $125.00 - $150.00.

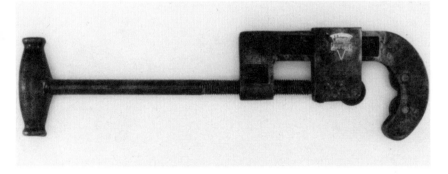

Pipe Cutter K2, three wheel pattern from ¼" to 2" capacity, $65.00 - $75.00.

Reamer K126 for reaming pipe and for counter sinking, $12.00 - $15.00.

Pipe Vise KP200 ⅛" to 2" capacity, 9¼" high; K312 Pipe Vise ⅛" to 3½" capacity, 11" high; $75.00 - $100.00 each.

# MISCELLANEOUS TOOLS

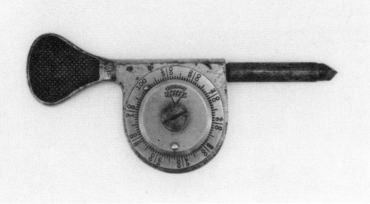

Speed Indicator K40 used to find speed of revolving axles or spindles on any kind of machinery, $75.00 - $85.00.

Screw Pitch Gauge, each leaf stamped showing pitch, $75.00 - $85.00.

Hand Grinder with 7" wheel, $100.00 - $125.00.

Tool Grinder, hand powered, $60.00 - $75.00.

Left: Oil Can, $40.00 - $50.00.
Right: Oil Stone with original cardboard box pictured on top and the stone, still with label, on the bottom, $35.00 - $40.00.

Left: Oil Bottle, clear, $15.00 - $20.00.
Middle: Oil Bottle, with original box, still has oil in it and has the paper label still on bottle, #K114, $65.00 - $75.00.
Right: Oil Bottles, two different blue bottles, $15.00 - $20.00 each.

Top: Marking Gauge, wooden, $20.00 - $25.00.
Middle: Marking Gauge, wooden with brass inserts, $35.00 - $40.00.
Bottom: Marking Gauge, K45 metal bar marking and mortise gauge, double ended, $60.00 - $65.00.

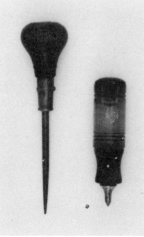

Scratch Awl, wooden handle with logo stamped in it, $35.00 - $45.00.

Scratch Awl, plastic handle, $15.00 - $20.00.

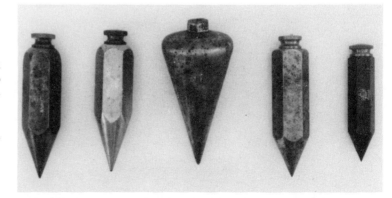

Plumb Bobs, logo varies on them, $45.00 - $65.00 each.
1st: 8 oz. hexagon          4th: 7 oz. hexagon steel
2nd: 7 oz. hexagon steel    5th: 3 oz. hexagon steel
3rd: 18 oz. round with screw top

51

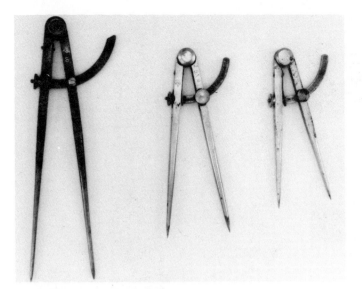

Dividers: K110, K108, K106, $35.00 - $45.00 each.

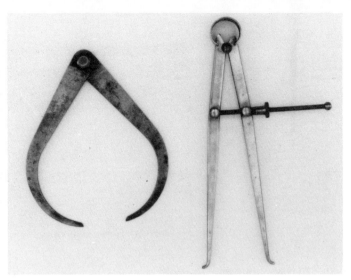

Left: K46 Outside Calipers, $35.00 - $40.00.
Right: K28 Inside Calipers, $35.00 - $40.00.

Carpenter Pencils: Set of twelve with wrapper (unused),
$120.00 - $150.00.
Carpenter Pencils: individual Shapleigh K107, Simmons
K109, and Shapleigh K109, $7.00 - $10.00 each.

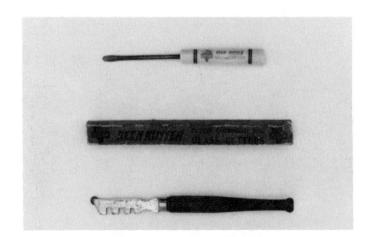

Screw Driver, displaying store advertisement,
$15.00 - $20.00.
Glass Cutter with original box, $35.00 - $40.00.

Nail Apron, $75.00.

Ship Carpenter's Adze KPS4,
$45.00 - $50.00.

Awl and Tool Set, ten tools with the same handle for all. Just slip in the tool you want and the rest go inside the handle and out of the way. $65.00 - $85.00.

Concrete Tools: Solid Brass
Top: Radius tool, $45.00 - $55.00.
Bottom: K01 Groover, $45.00 $55.00.

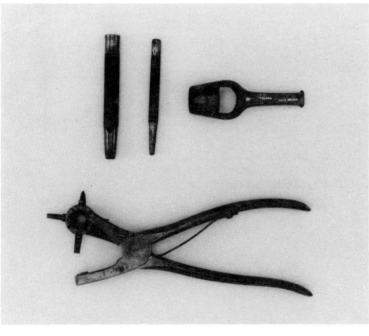

Left Photo:
Leather Punches, three different types, $8.00 - $12.00 each.
Revolving four-tube #K44 Punch, tube #'s 4, 6, 8, and 10, $35.00 - $40.00.

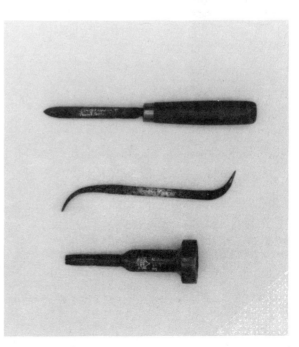

Right Photo:
Top: Bearing Scraper, $20.00 - $25.00.
Middle: Cotter Pin Lifter and Spreader combined, $20.00 - $25.00.
Bottom: Nut driver #5 for a brace, $15.00 - $20.00.

1st: K64 Linoleum Knife, 3½" blade, $12.00 - $18.00.
2nd: Shapleigh Linoleum Knife, $12.00 - $18.00.
3rd: K740 Linoleum Knife, 3" blade, $12.00 - $18.00.
4th: S1581AK Shapleigh Scraping Knife, $12.00 - $18.00.
5th: K75 Putty Knife, $12.00 - $18.00.

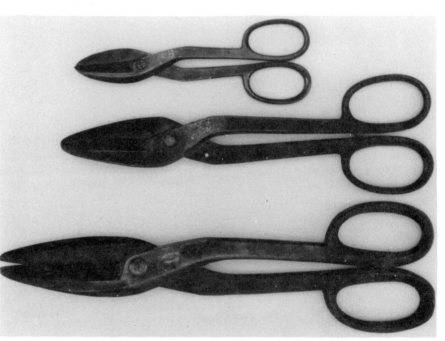

Top: Tinner Snips, $15.00 - $20.00.
Middle: K9 Tinners Snips, $15.00 - $20.00.
Bottom: K12 Tinner Snips, $15.00 - $20.00.

Nail Puller, 18" length, $35.00 - $40.00.

Carpenter's Wrecking Bars, goose neck, sizes 18", 24" and 30", $15.00 - $20.00 each.

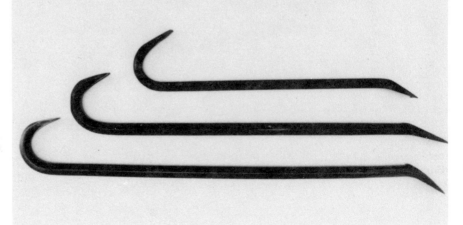

54

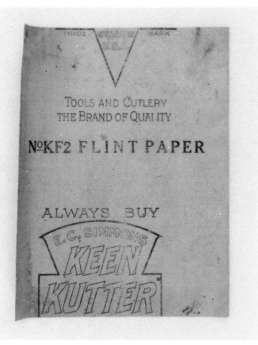

Flint Paper KF2, $8.00 - $10.00.

Emery Cloth, $6.00 - $8.00 per sheet.

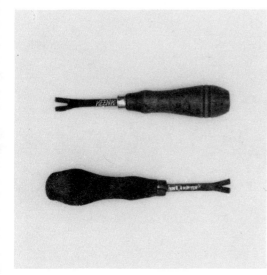

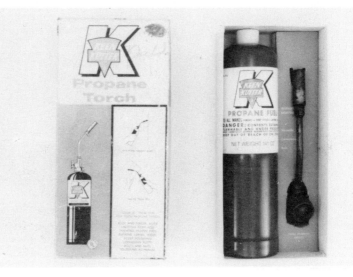

Tack Claws, both K5, $10.00 - $15.00 each.

Propane Torch, $35.00 - $45.00.

Boxes, five various wooden and cardboard, $10.00 - $25.00.

# AXES AND HATCHETS

Broad Axe, large logo, $100.00 - $125.00.

Broad Axe, Keen Kutter written out, no logo, $75.00 - $100.00.

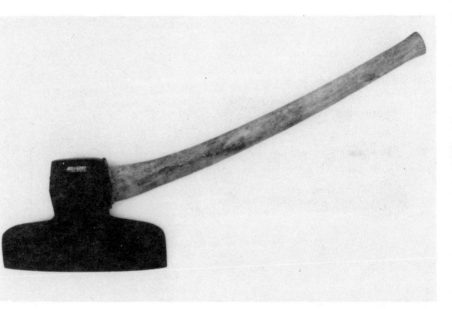

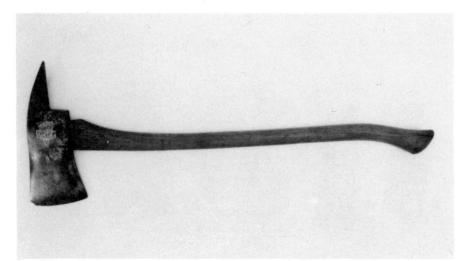

Fireman's Axe, $75.00 - $100.00.

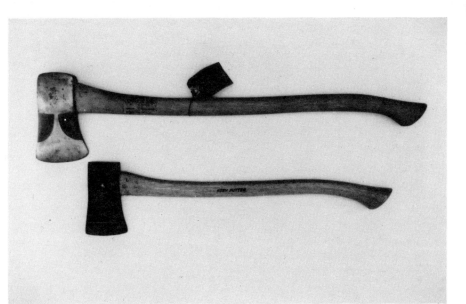

Axe, Michigan pattern, perfect bevel, with Cumberland handle, mint condition with original marked handle, $40.00 - $50.00.

Boy's Hand Axe, Michigan pattern, mint condition with original marked handle, $40.00 - $50.00.

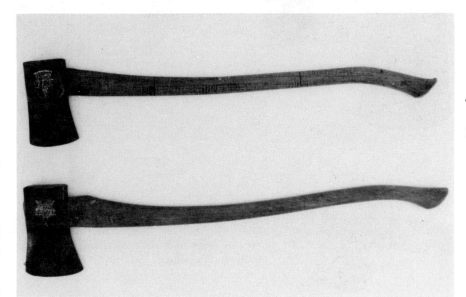

Top: Axe, New Yankee pattern, $20.00 - $25.00.
Bottom: Axe, Dayton wide head pattern plain, $20.00 - $25.00.

Top: Axe #5 special composite pattern plain, $20.00 - $25.00.

Bottom: Axe #KMA1 Michigan pattern with octagon handle and round head, $20.00 - $25.00.

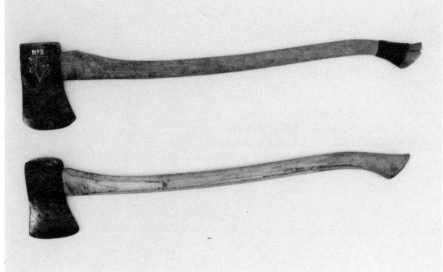

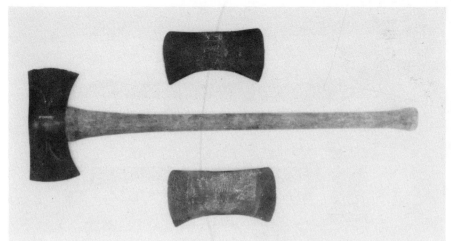

Top: Axe, double bit #50 stamped above large logo, $25.00 - $30.00.
Middle: Axe, double bit, special composite pattern with Keen Kutter written out, $15.00 - $20.00.
Bottom: Double bit axe, Kon-Kave written out above large logo, $25.00 - $30.00.

Sport Axe: Shapleigh, octagon handle still has Keen Kutter written on it. Axe has the duck flying off scene with "For Sportsman" written under it. $125.00 - $150.00.

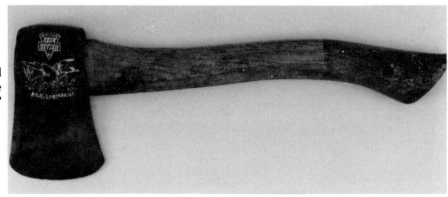

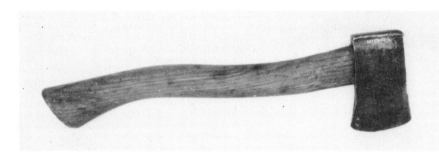

Hatchet, 2½" wide, 4" long head, small child size hatchet has Keen Kutter written on one side and E.C. Simmons, St. Louis, MO on the other. $75.00 - $100.00

Broad or Bench Hatchets:
3" to 4" size: $25.00 - $30.00 each.
5" to 6" size: $45.00 - $55.00 each.

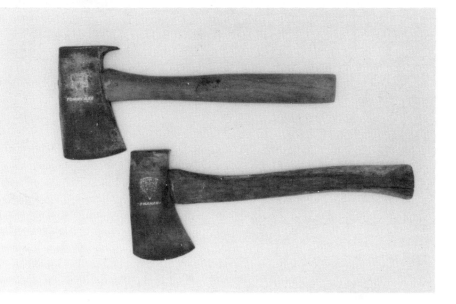

Top: Tommy Axe   $55.00 - $65.00
Bottom: Tomahawk Belt Axe
         $55.00 - $65.00

Top: Hunters Axe   $20.00 - $25.00.
Bottom: Scout Axe (has notch in it)
         $20.00 - $25.00.

Top: Lathing Hatchet has Keen Kutter
    written out, $20.00 - $25.00.
Bottom: Hunters Axe with Keen Kutter
    written out, $20.00 - $25.00.

Top: Rig Builders Hatchet, $20.00 - $25.00.
Bottom: Machinist Pattern Hatchet, $20.00 - $25.00.

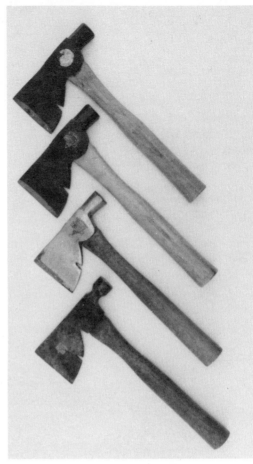

Top: Half Hatchet with original sticker, mint condition, $40.00 - $60.00.
2nd: Half Hatchet, mint, same as top without sticker, $40.00 - $60.00.
3rd: Half Hatchet, chrome-plated, $35.00 - $40.00.
4th: Half Hatchet, hammer head with small logo, $20.00 - $25.00.

Top: Claw Hatchet, Shapleigh, plain poll,
    $20.00 - $25.00.
2nd: Lathing Hatchet, $20.00 - $25.00.
3rd: Scout Axe, $20.00 - $25.00.
4th: Scout, steel shank with red rubber handle,
    $20.00 - $25.00.

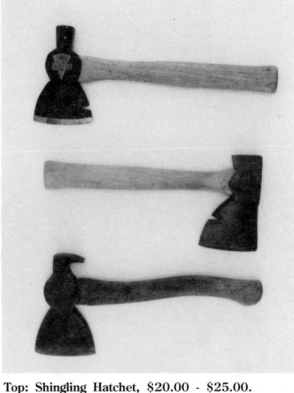

Top: Shingling Hatchet, $20.00 - $25.00.
Middle: Flooring Hatchet with nail slot,
    $20.00 - $25.00.
Bottom: Claw Hatchet, plain poll, $20.00 - $25.00.

60

Top: Lathing Hatchet, $18.00 - $25.00.
Bottom: Lathing Hatchet, square head, checkered
    face, $18.00 - $25.00.

Top: Produce Hatchet, genuine Underhill
    California pattern, $20.00 - $25.00.
Bottom: Produce Hatchet with special top
    nail slot, square checkered face,
    $20.00 - $25.00.

Left Photo:
Top: Hatchet Wedge - the head of every Keen
    Kutter hammer is fastened to the handle
    by a Keen Kutter patented lock wedge as
    pictured and will not fly off.  No value on
    this piece, just for information purposes.

Bottom: Hatchet Gauge #S20, $20.00.

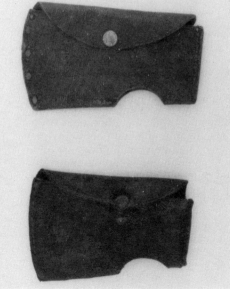

Right Photo:
Hatchet Sheaths, $20.00 - $25.00
each.

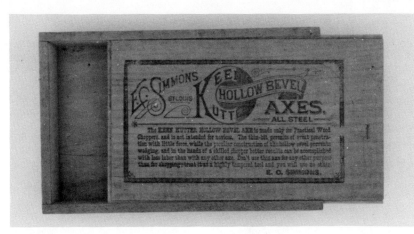

Axe Box, sliding top, 4½# hollow bevel axe head came in this, $25.00 - $35.00.

Axe Box, dove tailed, $15.00 - $20.00.

Axe Box, $10.00 - $15.00.

Axe Box: axe heads without handles were shipped in these.   $10.00 - $15.00.

# POCKET KNIVES

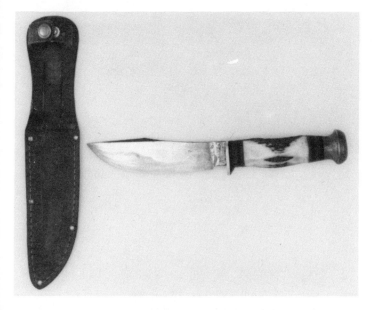

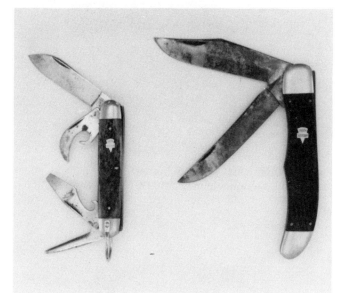

Hunting Knife, stage handle with colored fibre and brass washers. Polished aluminum guard and knob. Length of blade 5", overall length 9", marked on blade, has leather sheath. $150.00 - $200.00.

Left: Scout Knife #843, $60.00 - $85.00.
Right: Outdoor Knife #658, with stag handle. $60.00 - $85.00.

Switch Blade Knife, U.S. Patents of Dec. 21, 1909 and Sept. 13, 1910, $175.00 - $225.00.

Office Knife, 3¾" two large blades, white celluloid handle, etching on handle, #K02220 (Mint), $95.00.

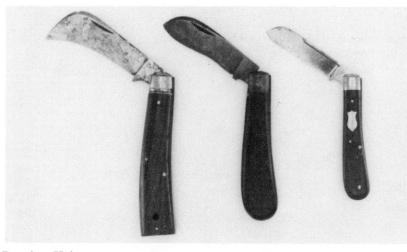

Key Chain Knife, $40.00 - $45.00.

Pruning Knives:
1st: KS105 Cocobolo handle; 4⅜" length extra heavy, $25.00 - $35.00.
2nd: KS106 Cocobolo handle, 4" length, $25.00 - $35.00.
3rd: Cocobolo handle, 3½" length (mint), $55.00 - $65.00.

Pocket Knife, #K1787 embossed iron handle black enameled, 3½" one blade, $60.00 - $90.00.

Pocket Knife, #K210SS, 3⅜" Cocobolo handle with chain, $60.00 - $75.00.

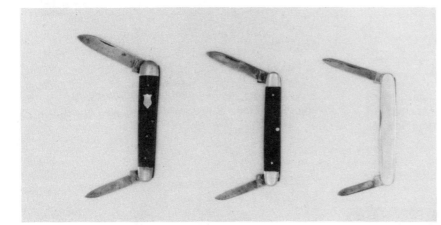

Pocket Knives, Two-Bladed:
Left: K0198, 3⅜" stag handle
Middle: K21 regular pen knife
Right: K0814, 3" nickel silver handle

Prices range from $25.00 - $60.00 depending on the condition.

Pocket Knives, Two-Bladed:
1st: Green celluloid handle
2nd: K02235N, 3" silvelour finish celluloid handle, gold glitter
3rd: Celluloid red and cream
4th: K233 celluloid red and cream

Prices range from $25.00 - $60.00 depending on the condition.

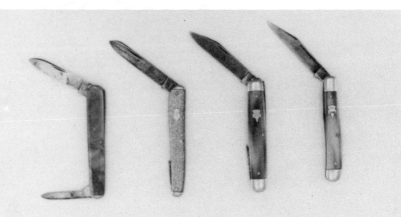

Vest Pocket Knives:
Left: K19
Middle 0214TK
Right: K18

Prices range from $20.00 - $60.00 depending on the condition.

Pocket Knives, Two-Bladed:
Left: The number is not legible,
     has black handle.
Middle: K53 ¾ stag handle 3⅜"
Right: #765 yellow handle

Prices range from $20.00 - $65.00 depending
on condition.

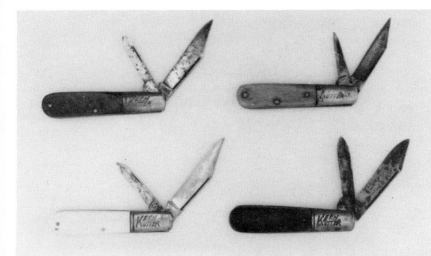

Pocket Knives, Barlow Pattern:
Top Left: #882 black bone handle
Bottom Left: K2884 ¾ white celluloid
           handle 3¼"
Top Right: K254 brown bone handle 3¼"
Bottom Right: K2881 ¾ bone handle clip
           point 3⅜"

Price range from $25.00 - $60.00 depending
on the condition.

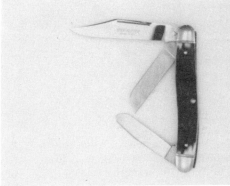

Left: #773 Congress Knife with four blades
Right: #767 Congress Knife with two blades
Prices range from $20.00 - $60.00 depending on the condition.

Pocket Knife, three bladed, #881, handmade. One
of the last Keen Kutter made by Shapleigh (mint).
$100.00 - $125.00.

Pocket Knives, three-bladed, Premium stock:
1st: K12 white nu-pearl celluloid handle
2nd: #861 stag handle
3rd: #886 stag handle

Prices range from $25.00 - $65.00 depending
on the condition.

Pocket Knives, Three-bladed:
1st: Red and cream color
2nd: Black handle
3rd: #793 (small) yellow handle
Prices range from $25.00 - $60.00 depending on the condition.

Pocket Knife, Three-bladed. No value placed on this knife. I just wanted to show how much this knife has been used.

Pocket Knife, Indian Design, sterling silver handle, #K4840SS (blade is broken). Condition as is $30.00 - $40.00.

Pocket Knife Box, $10.00 - $12.00. Pocket Knife Sharpening Stone, $10.00.

Knives made by Schrade Walden - Reproductions:
1st: K825RBKK stainless SS825 Schrade Walden, $25.00 - $35.00.
2nd: Article on 825RB
3rd: K1080T KK handmade Old Timer Schrade NY, $25.00 - $35.00.

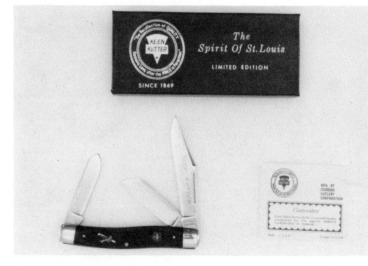

Spirit of St. Louis #K74, Limited Edition, Reproduction Knife.
12,000 were made in the USA; this one has serial number 4352. $35.00 - $55.00.

# RAZORS

Sign: Cardboard advertising Safety Razor, 10" high, 22" wide, color red/white/blue, $90.00 - $100.00.

Left: Safety razor with metal handle, $15.00 - $20.00.
Right: Junior Safety Razor with metal handle, $15.00 - $20.00.

Safety Razors, all different styles with original boxes, $10.00 - $20.00 each.

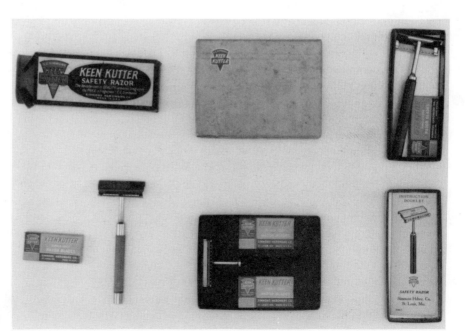

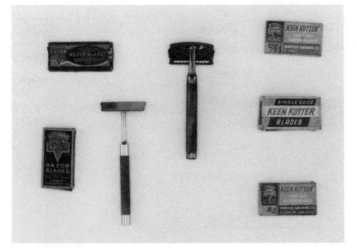

Razor Blade Packages all different, all containing blades, $2.00 - $6.00 per pack.

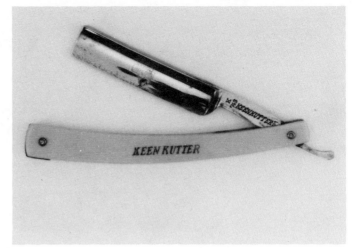

Straight Razor, K743 white celluloid handle with words Keen Kutter stamped in red, logo type letters on the front, etched in gold, full crocus polished blade. $25.00 - $35.00.

Straight Razor Box
1st Razor: Germany, metal handle with Keen Kutter written on back. Front has women in a full gown. $75.00 - $100.00.
2nd Razor: Logo etched in gold on blade plus Mother of Pearl on end of blade. $55.00 - $65.00.
3rd Razor: K419 ¾ concaved blade edged in gold, $20.00 - $25.00.

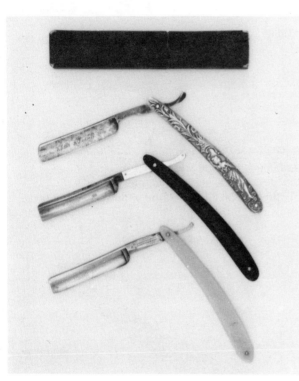

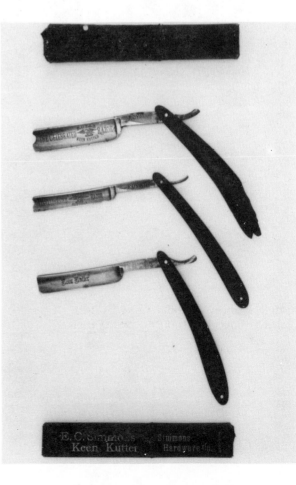

Top: Straight razor "The Celebrated" ¾" blade (has busted handle), $20.00 - $25.00.
Middle: Straight razor "The Celebrated" ½" blade, black handle, $20.00 - $25.00.
Bottom: #1150, one of the first straight razors, has Keen Kutter written on the blade, ⅝" blade, $20.00 - $25.00.

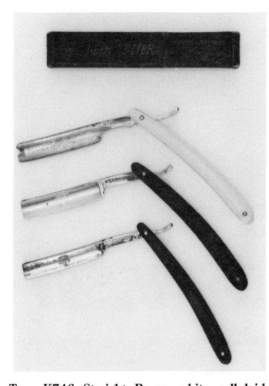

Left: KK Junior Razor Hone with aluminum box and instructions, $25.00 - $35.00.
Middle: K20 Razor Hone in metal box with instructions, $25.00 - $35.00.
Top Right: K15 Razor Hone with a cardboard box, $25.00 - $35.00.
Bottom Right: K15 Razor Hone with its cardboard box shown open, $25.00 - $35.00.

Top: K746 Straight Razor, white celluloid handle, full concave blade edged in gold, full crocus polished, $20.00 - $35.00.
Middle: K44 Straight Razor, plain black rubber handle, ¾ concaved blade, file tang, edged in gold, $20.00 - $35.00.
Bottom: K13 Straight Razor, gold inlaid logo, $20.00 - $35.00.

Corn Razors, one has a celluloid handle and the other has a black rubber handle marked Germany. $35.00 - $45.00 each with box.

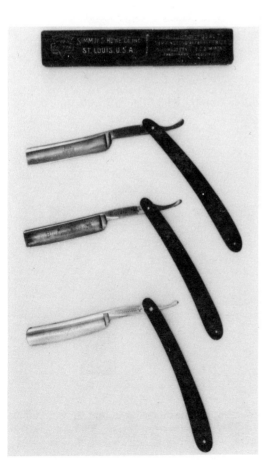

Top: K15 Straight Razor, black handle with logo in center of handle and on blade, $25.00 - $35.00.
Middle: K15 Straight Razor, blue steel with logo in center of handle and on blade, $25.00 - $35.00.
Bottom: K16 Straight Razor, blue steel with logo in center of handle and on blade, $25.00 - $35.00.

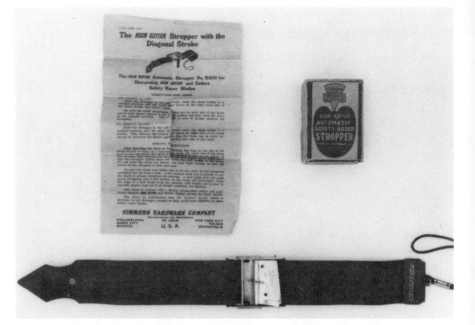

K600 Automatic Safety Razor Stropper in original box with instructions, $40.00 - $45.00.

Razor Strop, K50 Cushion Comb, $45.00 - $55.00.

Left: K80 Razor Strop, combination double swing, 24" length, 2½" width, $25.00.
Right: K94 Razor Strop, professional combination, double swing, 24" length, 2½" width, $30.00 - $35.00.

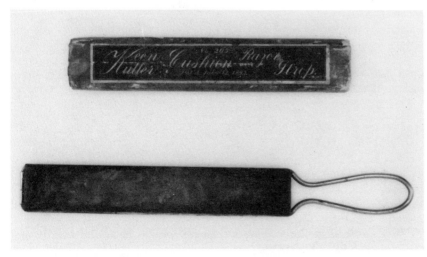

Razor Strop #205, Pat'd July 12, 1892, has original cover. $40.00 - $45.00.

Shaving Containers: one for soap and the other for the shaving brush, $15.00 - $20.00 pair.

# SCISSORS AND SHEARS

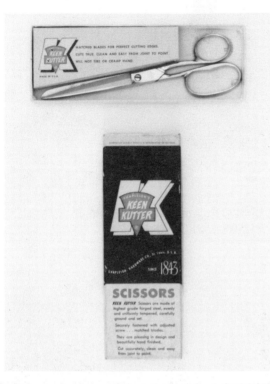

Scissor box containing the original S128AK scissor, $50.00 - $55.00.

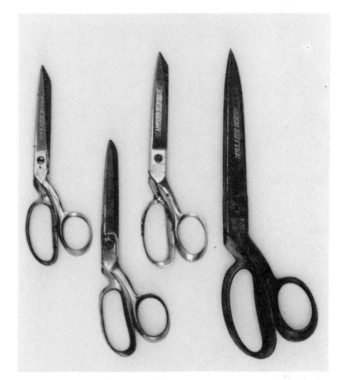

Scissors from left to right:
6½" scissors, $6.00 - $10.00.
7½" scissors, $6.00 - $10.00.
7" scissors (double stamped Keen Kutter/Diamond Edge), $6.00 - $10.00.
10" scissors, $6.00 - $10.00.

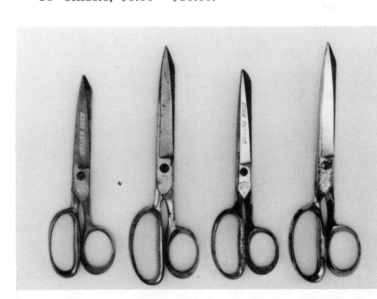

Shears - E.C. Simmons:
7" and 8" chrome, $6.00 - $10.00 each.
7" and 8" black handle, $6.00 - $10.00 each.

Scissors box (empty), $10.00 - $15.00.
Paper Shears, $15.00 - $20.00.
Shears box (empty), $10.00 - $15.00.

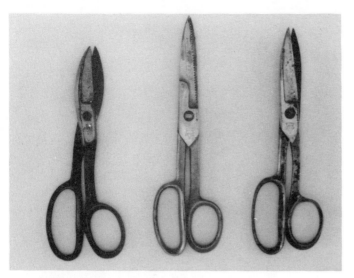

Left: Dental or Factory Snips   $12.00 - $15.00
Middle: K5 Kitchen Shears   $12.00 - $15.00
Right: K11D Dental Snips   $12.00 - $15.00

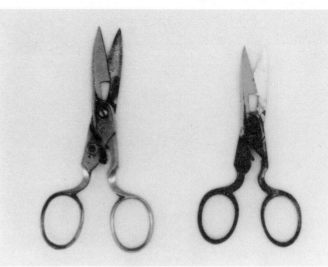

Button Hole Scissors, two different styles.
$15.00 - $20.00 each.

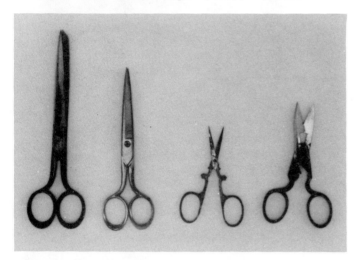

Scissors from left to right:   7" Scissors, $5.00 - $7.00;
5½" Scissors, $5.00 - $7.00;   3½" Scissors, fancy style,
$15.00 - $20.00;   4¼" Germart button hole, $15.00 -
$20.00.

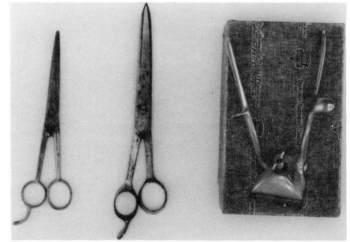

Barbers' Shears, 8½", $8.00 - $10.00.
Barbers' Shears, 7", $8.00 - $10.00.
Hair Clippers, K543 with original box, $30.00 - $35.00.

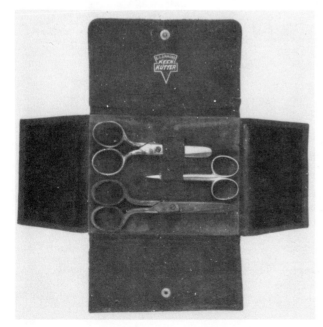

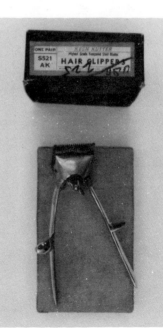

Left Photo:
Scissors in carrying case,
$45.00 - $55.00.

Right Photo:
Hair Clippers, S521AK in
original box, $25.00 - $30.00.

72

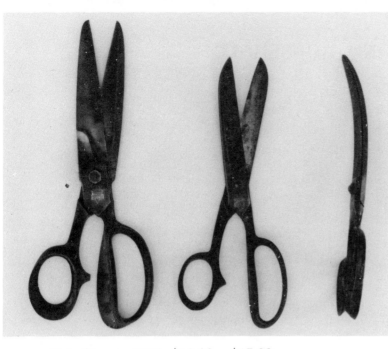

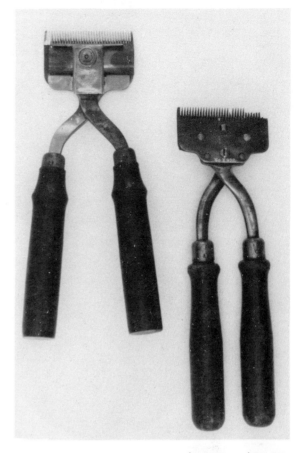

Mule Shears, 10½", $12.00 - $15.00.
Roaching Shears, 9¼", $12.00 - $15.00.
Roaching Shears, 9", side view, $12.00- $15.00.

Left: Horse Clippers #K940, $15.00 - $20.00.
Right: Horse Clippers #K920, $15.00 - $20.00.

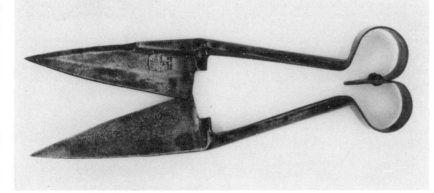

Sheep Shears, has unusual engraving on them of a man shearing sheep, marked "Made In England."   $45.00 - $50.00.

Mule Shears #K100, $10.00 - $15.00.

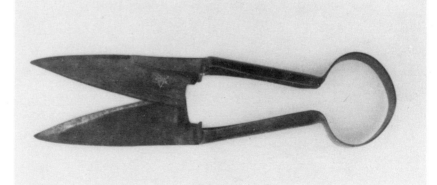

**Left and Top Photos:**
Waffle Iron, cast iron with four sections, 7¼" cake size with Keen Kutter logo written in, E.C. Simmons embossed on lid, low base type. (This is being reproduced.) Original, per photo, $125.00 - $175.00.
Above, photo of a waffle we made on this waffle iron.

**Right and Bottom Photos: Waffle Iron - Reproduction (small).** These started surfacing the first part of 1988. They are copied identical to the original one that has the E.C. Simmons logo inside with the exception of the size being 3⅞" griddle size and the handle is wooden. The original handle is the wire twist look. Some people are selling these by calling them salesman samples. Until these surfaced, I hadn't heard of a salesman sample waffle iron. They are selling as low as $15.00 and some are being passed at outrageous prices by being sold as original. BEWARE!

Apple Parer, patent date May 24, 1898. It pares the entire apple and ejects it, $60.00 - $75.00.

Waffle Iron, cast iron, has four sections with small logo, cake size 6¼", low base type, Simmons embossed on lid, $125.00 - $175.00.

Kraut Cutter, single 9" blade x 26½", patent date October 1904, cast iron logo on side and Keen Kutter marked on top, $65.00 - $75.00.

Kraut Cutter, single 8" blade x 26½", only marked with emblem on sliding box, $65.00 - $75.00.

Kraut Cutter, $65.00 - $75.00.

Left: Star Mincers with 6 blades,
    $10.00 - $20.00.
Middle: KBB Mincing Knife, single blade,
    $10.00 - $20.00.
Right: Mincing Knife, double-bladed,
    $10.00 - $20.00.

Butcher's Chopper, $30.00 - $35.00.
Household Cleaver, $25.00 - $30.00.

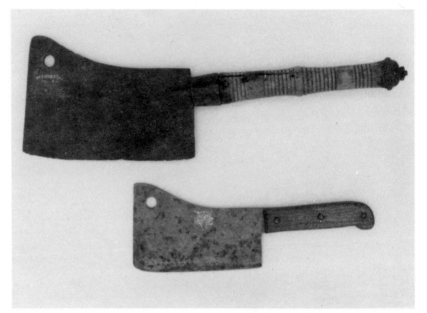

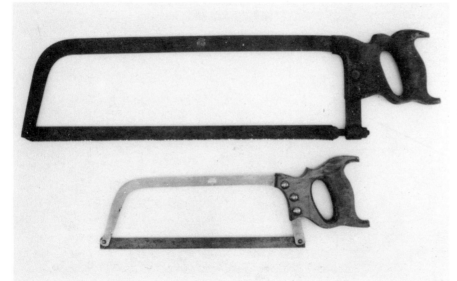

Top: Butcher Saw K15 with 20" blade,
    $35.00 - $40.00.
Bottom: Kitchen Saw K2 with 14" blade,
    $35.00 - $40.00.

Butcher Saw Blades, 25 ft. coil of continuous blade. You would cut your desired length to use in butcher saw. #KF ¾ in the original box, $30.00 - $35.00.

Meat Grinder, K112 large family size with separate base plate, sliding base and thumb screw, $25.00 - $35.00.

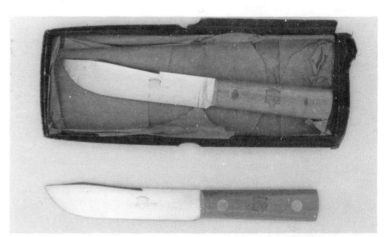

Butcher Knives, K160 6" in original box (mint), $20.00 each.

Meat Cutters, clamp-to-table models, K105 for family size and K110 for large family size, $15.00 - $20.00 each.

Top: 8" Slicer, swagged blade, $12.00 - $15.00.
Middle: K10 Cook's Knife 8", $15.00 - $20.00.
Bottom: Butcher Knife with logo, $12.00 - $16.00.

Top: Roast Beef Slicer, 12", $15.00 - $20.00.
Middle: K52 Ham Slicer, 10" long,
$15.00 - $20.00.
Bottom: K334 Bread Knife, 10" blade,
$15.00 - $20.00.

Knife Steels: All three have the emblem
for the guard. Lengths 10", 12" and 14",
$25.00 - $35.00 each.

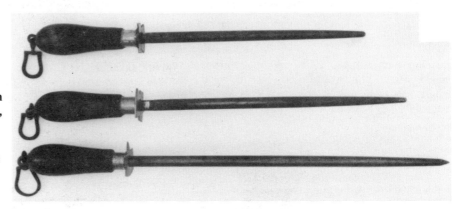

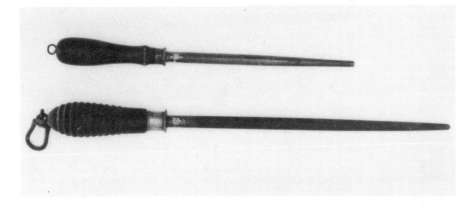

Top: K540 8" Knife Steel,
$15.00 -$20.00.
Bottom: 12" Knife Steel, $10.00 - $12.00.

Carving Set, three piece (knife, fork, steel)
with stag handles, sterling silver ferrules
with nickel silver caps with logo on them,
$45.00 - $55.00.

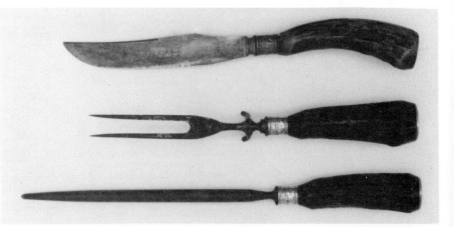

78

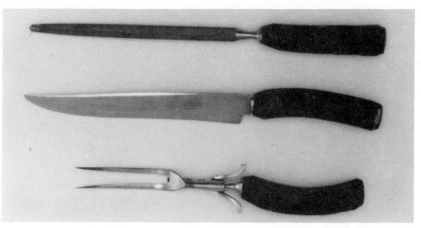

Carving Set, three piece with stag handles, hollow bolsters and nickel silver caps, $35.00 - $45.00.

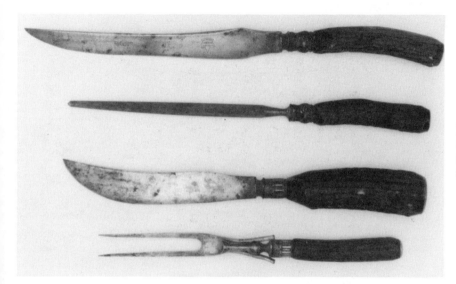

Knife & Steel (two piece) stag handles, $20.00 - $25.00.
Carving Set (two piece) stag handles, $25.00 - $35.00.

Steak or Chop Carver, two piece, stag handles with sterling silver ferrules with logo on them, $45.00 - $50.00.

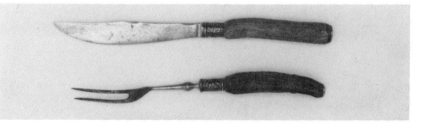

Table Cutlery, silver plate set with six knives and six forks in original box, $65.00 - $75.00.

79

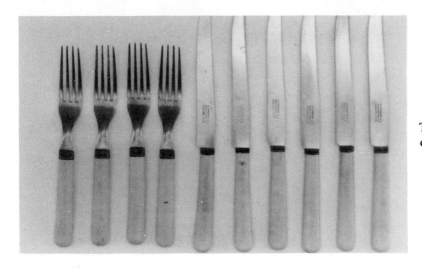

Tableware, four forks and six knives with yellow celluloid handles, $45.00.

Butter Knives, six with celluloid handles, $35.00 - $45.00.

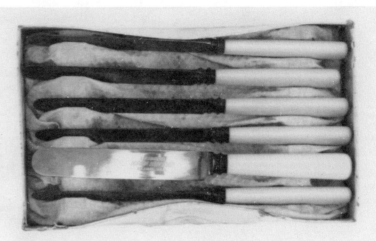

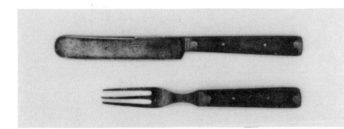

Table Cutlery, two piece, wooden handles, $10.00 set.

Top: Table Knife, stag handle, $8.00.
Middle: Table Knife, bone handle, $8.00.
Bottom: Table Knife, K2520 Cocobolo handle with two pins, $8.00.

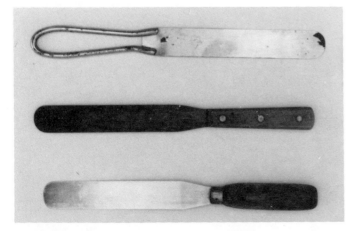

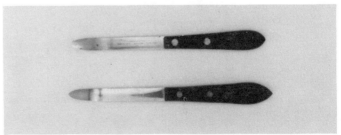

Top: Spatula, all metal, $12.00 - $15.00.
Middle: K646/7 Spatula 7" blade, $12.00 - $15.00.
Bottom: K366 Spatula 7" blade, $12.00 - $15.00.

Grape Fruit Knives, 3¼" long, serrated double edge curved blade, $8.00 - $12.00 each.

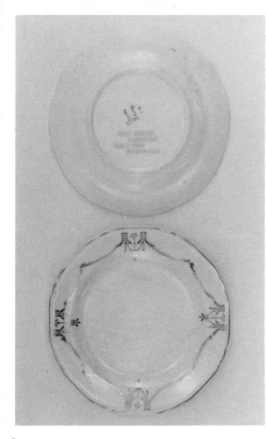

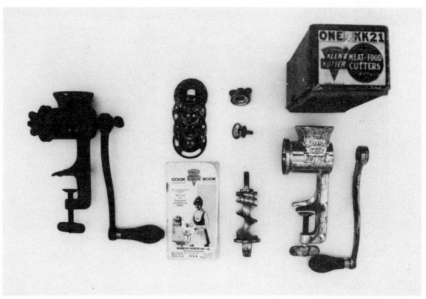

Food Chopper, K21 with original box and cookbook, $30.00 - $35.00.
Food Chopper, K10, $10.00 - $15.00.

**Saucers: two saucers**

Photo shows one view of the back and one view of the front. This is Polly Prime Housewares, semi-porcelain chinaware #290 series. Ivory body with dainty chain design and double tracing finished with novelty effect at the edges. Each saucer has Keen Kutter written on the back. These are the only pieces of this pattern I have been able to find. $10.00 each.

Food Choppers, K22½ and K23, $10.00 - $15.00 each.

Food Chopper, K22 Simmons with original box and cookbook, $30.00 - $35.00.

Food Chopper, K22 Shapleigh with original box and cookbook, tightening knobs are aluminum, $30.00 - $35.00.

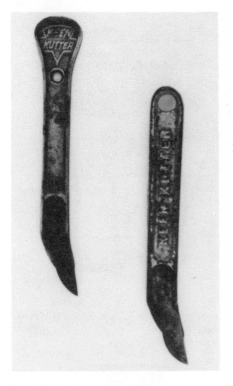

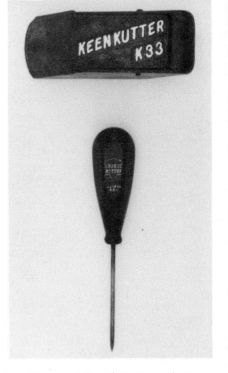

Can Openers, two different types, $15.00 - $20.00 each.

Cork Screws, three different types, $15.00 each.

Ice Shaver K33, $65.00 - $75.00. Ice Pick, $45.00 - $50.00.

Water Jug, Shapleigh, insulated, faucet type, $75.00 - $100.00.

Tobacco Cutter, base marked "E.C. Simmons" St. Louis, U.S.A. $175.00 - $250.00.

Cordless Rechargeable Knife, a later model, no manufacturer name, just has Keen Kutter written on it, $45.00.

Corn Mill Grinder, cast iron, $65.00 - $75.00.

Sewing Machine:
One photo shows the lid open, and the other with the lid closed. Volo Threadle Machine marked E.C. Simmons on the peddle.

The key holes in the drawers have the brass Keen Kutter logo for keyhole covers. It has a brass Keen Kutter key as well as a small screw driver marked Keen Kutter. $200.00 - $300.00.

# YARD AND GARDEN TOOLS

Left Photo: Advertisement found in Saturday Evening Post, May 8, 1909 issue, $10.00 - $15.00.

Top Photo: Wheelbarrow, $125.00 - $175.00.

Left:
Lawn Mower, push type, wood handle, $30.00 - $40.00.

Right:
Lawn Mower, push type, chrome caps and metal handles, $30.00 - $40.00.

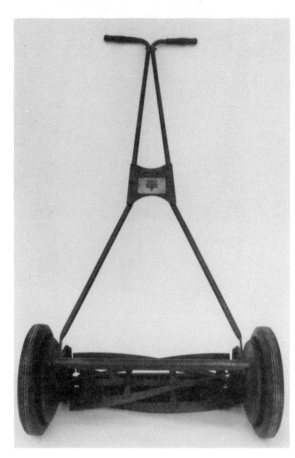

Left:
Lawn Mower,
push type, has metal
handle,
$30.00 - $40.00.

Right:
Lawn Mower,
gasoline power,
$65.00 - $85.00.

Spark Plug, manufactured for Val-Test Dist. Chicago, IL., fits a K17M power mower, $40.00 - $50.00.

Gas Cans, two different styles of the 2½ gallon capacity, $20.00 - $25.00 each.

Gas Can, five-gallon capacity, $30.00 - $35.00.

Gas Cans, two different styles of the one-gallon capacity, $15.00 - $20.00 each.

Grass Shears, four different types shown, $10.00 - $15.00 each.

Pruning Shears, three different types shown, $15.00 - $20.00.

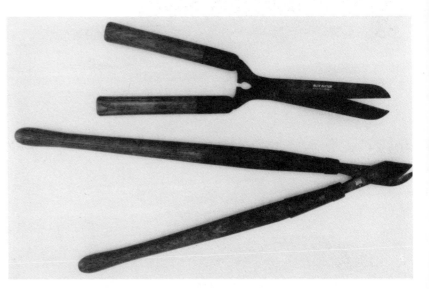

Top: Hedge Shears #KS8½, $15.00 - $20.00.
Bottom: Pruning Shears, $20.00 - $25.00.

Bush Scythe, 18", mint with paper sticker, $40.00.  If used, $10.00 - $15.00.

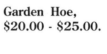

Weed Cutter #KWCS - K, $25.00 - $30.00.

Dandelion Weeder, $25.00 - $30.00.

Garden Hoe, $20.00 - $25.00.

Bush Hook $30.00 - $40.00 Ditch Bank Blade, socket pattern, 71" overall length, $30.00 - $40.00.

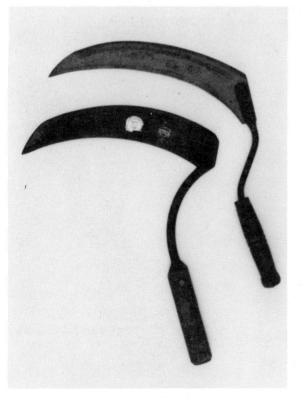

Grass Hooks, two different types, $15.00 - $20.00 each.

Eye Hoe - wide, scovil pattern planter, $35.00 - $45.00.
Eye Hoe - long, sprouting, $35.00 - $45.00.

Grub Hoe, $25.00 - $30.00.

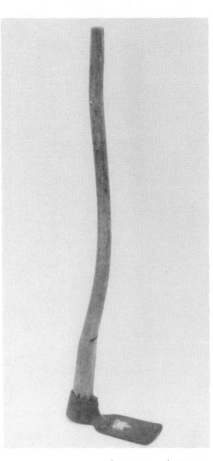

Eye Hoe 4½" cut, $20.00 - $25.00.

Weeding Hoe K3C4½, $25.00 - $30.00.

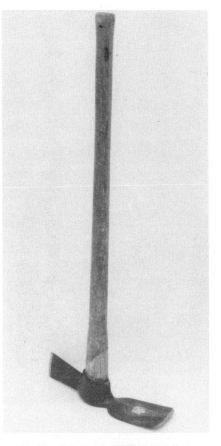

Cutter Mattock #KM, medium cutter, $35.00 - $40.00.

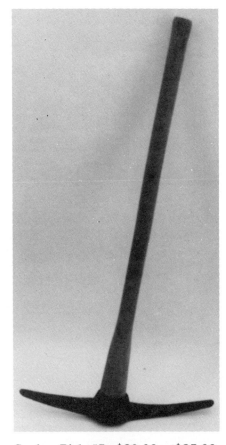

Garden Pick #5, $20.00 - $25.00.

Garden Mattock Hoe #KHM dig-ezy pattern, $35.00 - $40.00.

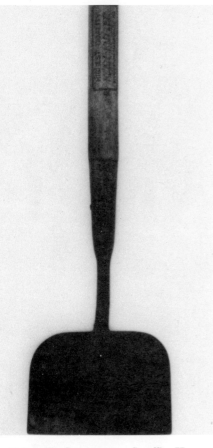

Sidewalk Scraper or Scuffle Hoe,
$25.00 - $30.00.

Mortar Hoe #KPM10,
$20.00 - $25.00.

Garden Rake with 12 teeth,
$20.00 - $25.00.

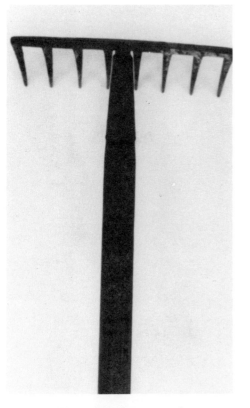

Floral Rake KR8, $25.00 - $30.00.

Dandelion Rake, socket pattern
#KLDR.  The saw teeth would
exterminate dandelions by cutting off the blossoms.
$15.00 - $20.00.

Shovels, round point and square point,
$15.00 - $20.00 each.

Left Photo:
Scoupe Shovel, all wood handle, $30.00 - $40.00.
Shovel #KRD2B, $25.00 - $30.00.

Right Photo:
Spades: Two different post or ditching spades and a regular dirt spade, $20.00 - $25.00 each.

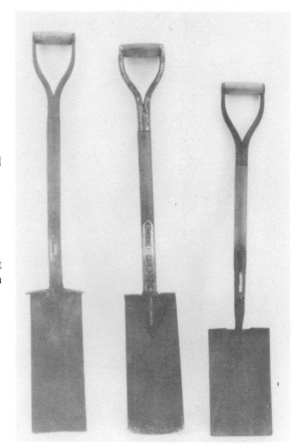

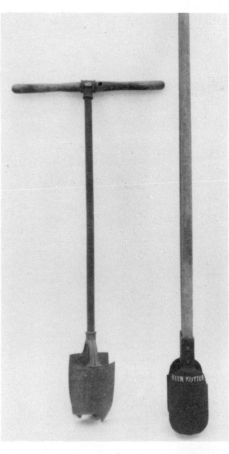

Dirt Shovel, wood handle, square point, $30.00 - $40.00.
Dirt Shovel, regular metal handle, square point, $20.00 - $25.00.

Garden Trowel #K2 socket pattern with bent neck, $10.00 - $15.00.

Post Hole Auger, $35.00 - $45.00.
Post Hole Digger, $20.00 - $25.00.

90

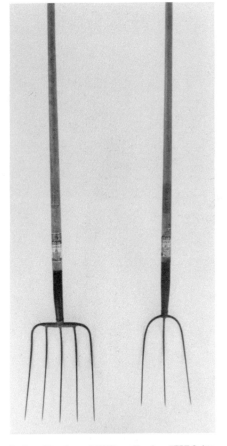 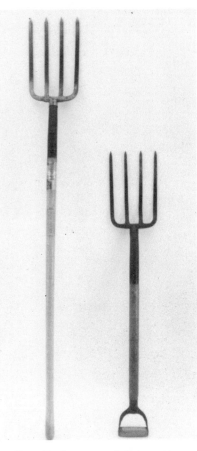 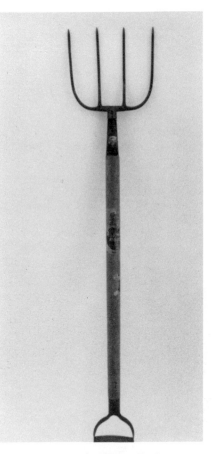

Left: Barley Utility Fork #K504½, five tine, $18.00 - $22.00.
Right: Hay Fork #KB304½, three tine, $15.00 - $20.00.

Spading Forks, two different types, one has a long bent handle, $15.00 - $20.00 each.

Barn or Ensilage Fork, $30.00 - $35.00.

Left Photo:
Left: KSC4 Speedy Cultivator, $20.00 - $25.00.
Right: K4BOL Potato Hook, $20.00 - $25.00.

Right Photo:
Baling Press Fork #KHB44½, $25.00 - $30.00.

# FARM TOOLS

Right Photo:
Post Drill #K1902, $150.00 - $200.00.

Bottom Photo:
Vise #KM400 has 4" jaws, $150.00 - $200.00.

Grinder, sit down style, $100.00 - $150.00.

Sickle & Tool Grinder, $55.00 - $65.00.

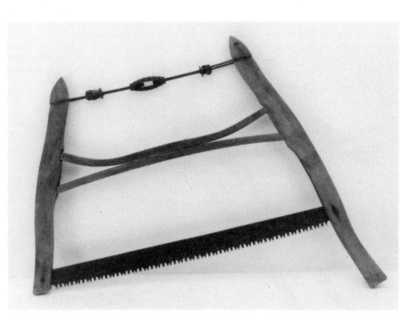

Hay Knife, straight or Heath's Pattern, $75.00 - $100.00.

Buck Saw, emblem on wood part, right side, $85.00 - $100.00.

One-Man Cross Cut Saw #309 with emblem on the blade, $75.00 - $100.00.

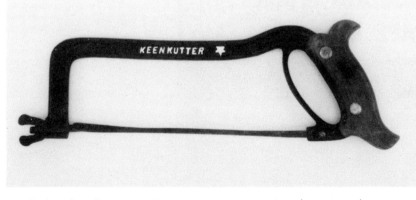

Dehorning Saw, cast iron with wood handle, $35.00 - $40.00.

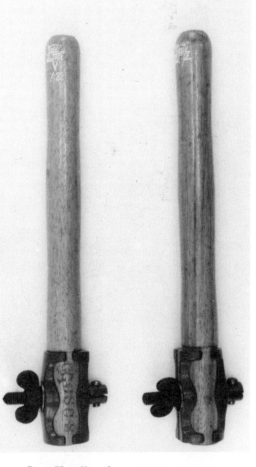

Saw Handles for a two-man saw, $20.00 - $25.00 pair.

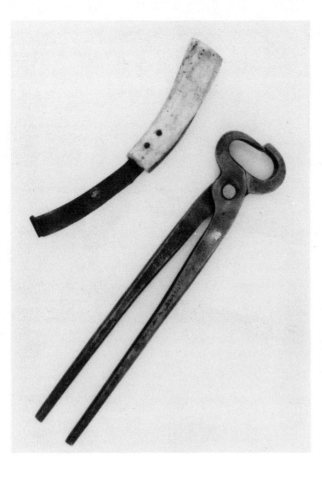

Left Photo:
Hoof Paring Pincers 12", $10.00 - $12.00.
Farriers Knife with a bone handle, $50.00 - $65.00.

Bottom Photo:
Spoke Pointers, two different sizes pictured, $40.00 - $45.00 each.

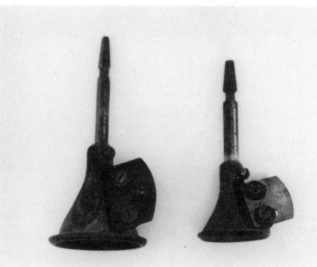

# ADVERTISING

Porclein Emblem Sign, two-sided, size 1', went on the side of buildings or stores. This sign has some chips. Mint $200.00 - $250.00.

Hardware Advertising Signs, 9¾" x 27¾", tin signs used on buildings, fences, etc. Each has the store name and location carrying Keen Kutter products. Very colorful - white, black, red, dark green and light green, $25.00 - $35.00 each.

Neon Sign, $450.00 - $500.00.

Sign, 24" x 48" yellow, white and red. Hardware store's name was to be placed on the white section under Keen Kutter. This one was never used. $100.00 - $110.00.

Hardware Sign, metal 29½" x 29½", white with blue outlines, emblem red with white lettering, $100.00 - $125.00.

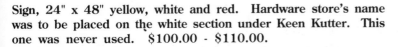

Electric Clock, E.C. Simmons, round window clock #KKEC. Red enameled 18¾" with a 15" white dial. This clock was given FREE to any dealer buying $300.00 or more of a single order of Keen Kutter products. If the dealer wanted, he could purchase the clock for $35.00 with the minimum order. $325.00 - $375.00.

Electric Clock, E.C. Simmons 15" x 15" square #K530. Purpose of this clock was to be placed in the store window to attract the attention of passersby who daily checked the time. $175.00 - $225.00.

Clock, Shapleigh, 10" round plastic with yellow, white and red color, $120.00 - $150.00.

Left Photo: Thermometer - AUTHENTIC - size 12", $120.00 - $130.00.
Right Photo: Thermometer - REPRODUCTION - Beware! Shapleigh's also. Biggest difference is the variance of temperature. The original only goes from -30° to 120° where the reproduction goes from -60° to 140°. The reproduction also has a smaller spring on the back. Reproduction sells for $12.00 - $15.00.

Thermometers, Indoor/Outdoor:
1st: Metal with wood back, size 2½" x 9",
     $45.00 - $65.00.
2nd: Metal with wood back, size 1¾" x 7½",
     $45.00 - $65.00.
3rd: Plastic bakelite back, size 2½" x 9".
     $45.00 - $65.00.

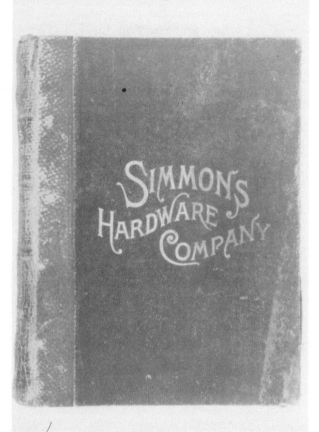

Simmons Hardware Company Catalog, January 20, 1899.   Leather bound, contains 1,712 pages, $400.00 - $450.00.

Salesman's Carrying Case
15" x 14" x 8½" for carrying catalogs and sales literature to hardware stores, $75.00 - $100.00.

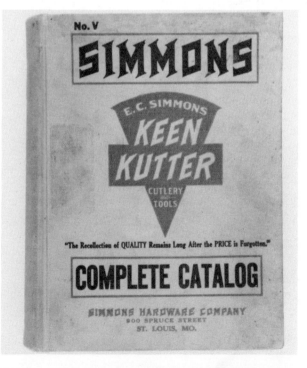

Catalog, 1935 Volume 5, Simmons Hardware Company.  Cover is yellow with red and black lettering, contains 2,118 pages.  $250.00 - $325.00.

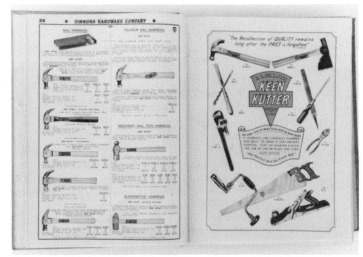

Statistics Page from the January 20, 1899 catalog listing the following interesting statistics in making the catalog possible:

Contains (including index) .......................... 1,768 Pages
Contains ............................................ 8,350 Illustrations
Entire Edition ...................................... 12,000 Copies
Each Copy Weighs ................................... 16 lbs.
Edition Weighs ..................................... 95 Tons
Paper Used ......................................... 6 Car Loads
Tar Boards Used In Binding ......................... 13½ Tons
Seal Grain Leather Used ............................ 11,000 Sq. Ft.
Cloth Used In Binding .............................. 24,000 Sq. Yd.
Time Consumed, Printing and Binding ........ 14 Months
Delivered in ....................................... 650 Packing Cases
Requiring .......................................... 110 Wagon Loads

A photo from the 1935 catalog opened to the tool section.

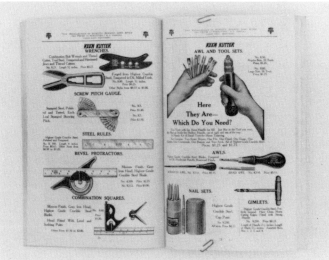

Salesman Catalog opened to show how Keen Kutter items were advertised.

Left Photo:
A photo of E.C. Simmons taken from the 1935 catalog.

Right Photo:
Catalog, 1939 Simmons. Black cover with red lettering, good shape, $150.00 - $200.00.

Left Photo:
Salesman Catalog containing nothing but Keen Kutter items. The cover has the salesman's name on it. Size is 6" x 9" with 104 pages, $300.00 - $350.00.

Right Photo:
Catalog, 1941 Shapleigh Keen Kutter/Diamond Edge. Contains 28 sections, 4" thick, cover black with orange lettering. Section 28 is a "Repair and Extra Parts Division" and was sent to the store only upon request. $150.00 - $200.00.

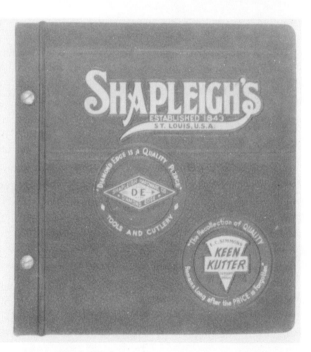

Mail Order Want Books, two are Simmons, color red, $25.00 - $35.00 each; other, Winchester-Simmons Company Keen Kutter, $25.00 - $35.00.

Left Photo:
Catalogs, five Specialty Item Catalogs. Color green and red. Categories include: Farm and Garden Tools, House Furnishing Goods, Spring and Summer Sporting Goods, Builders' Hardware, Tool Catalog.
Value $25.00 - $30.00 each. Set value, $125.00 - $175.00.

Top Photo:
Want Book, yellow E.C. Simmons. This went along with the 1935 catalog. $20.00 - $25.00.
Shapleigh's Mail Order/Want Books, color green, $15.00 - $20.00 each

Top Photo:
Post Card, advertising the Keen Kutter lawn mower, $25.00 - $35.00.

Right Photo:
Post Card, back view. "Like Velvet" from the Keen Kutter lawn mower post card.

Post Card: Keen Kutter sign hanging on a store front in Poplar Bluff, Missouri, $35.00 - $40.00.

Left Photo:
Top: Hardware Store Correspondence Card, used to contact the customer regarding an order. $15.00 - $20.00.

Bottom: Salesman Call Card telling when the salesman would be at the Hardware store. $15.00 - $20.00.

Pocket Calendar, 1912, also serves as a scratch pad, $20.00 - $25.00.

Trade Card: photos show front and back of this trade card. Front is hatchet head; back, "sales pitch" encouraging customer to buy Keen Kutter. $40.00 - $45.00.

**Keen Kutter Cutlery and Tools**

TROORLATPIF
"The recollection of quality remains long after the price is forgotten."
Trade Mark Registered.

Not what you pay but what you get for your money.
Get the "Keen Kutter Kwality"—found only in

If you get the habit of using only the best tools and cutlery, you will use the Keen Kutter brand. Quality uniformly the highest. Prices are the lowest for strictly high grade goods.

If you have had trouble in getting tools that would hold a keen edge, you have not been buying the best.

Keen Kutter goods are particularly made for USE by intelligent workmen, and will do good work under stress of hard usage longer than any other kind.
See Tools in our exhibit showing from ten to twenty years' wear.

SIMMONS HARDWARE COMPANY, INC.
MANUFACTURERS AND DISTRIBUTERS,
ST. LOUIS, MO., - - U.S.A.

(OVER)

101

Calendars, tin, pad type with hardware store name and location, $50.00 - $65.00 each.

Calendar, 1944, Girl with doll, $50.00 - $75.00.

Calendar, 1945, Westhoff Mercantile, Birth Of The Flag, $100.00 - $125.00.

Left Photo:
Calendar, 1949,
Licking Hardware,
Three Pointer Dogs,
$75.00 - $100.00.

Right Photo:
Calendar, 1953,
Herron Hardware,
Boy Fishing,
$50.00 - $75.00.

Left Photo:
Calendar, 1957,
Lake Of The West,
$50.00 - $75.00.

Right Photo:
Calendar, 1957,
Girl Praying,
$50.00 - $75.00.

Top of Each Photo:
Hand Fan: Front side is the hatchet and the back side is Keen Kutter Exhibit at the 1904 World's Fair in St. Louis. $75.00 - $90.00. (Handle is shaped like a hatchet handle.)

Bottom of Each Photo:
Hand Fan: Front side is of the Keen Kutter emblem and back side is advertising Williams Hardware Company and the Home Comers Week in Jackson, Missouri. $40.00 - $45.00.

Fan, hand held, front and back views. Front is Girl With Her Dog and the back is Wm. Clingingsmith Hardware. $40.00 - $45.00.

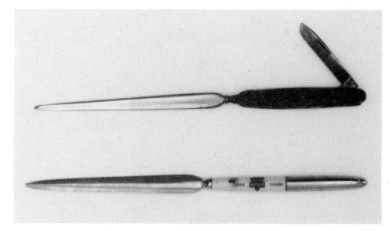

Fan: fold-up handheld fan with logo on one side and a floral design on the other, not pictured, $75.00 - $85.00.

Letter Openers:
Top: Has a knife blade and a leather cover, $30.00.
Bottom: Has a pen on the end and hardware store advertisement, $30.00.

Sliding Yard Sticks, seven different hardware company locations shown here. The bottom one shows the size when folded up. $15.00 - $20.00 each.

Yardsticks, all advertising different hardware stores, $10.00 - $15.00 each.

Left Photo:
Match Book, advertiser was Marien Hardware Co., Indianapolis, Phone: Garfield 7551, $10.00 - $12.00.

Right Photo:
Wrapping Paper with store advertising (pieces from the paper rolls). Small sheets as pictured, $4.00 - $6.00 each.

105

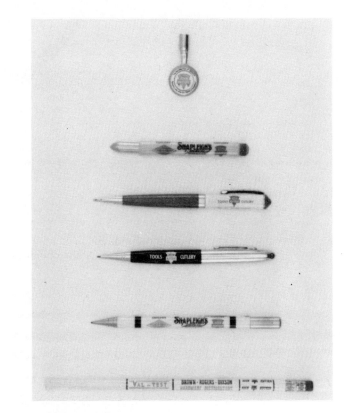

Pencil Clip, $5.00.
Bullet Pencil (Diamond Edge/Keen Kutter), $15.00.
Two Mechanical Pencils, $10.00 - $15.00 each.
Shapleigh DE/KK Mechanical Pencil,
$20.00 - $25.00.
Pencil, $5.00 - $6.00.

Invoice, 1906, E.C. Simmons, shows the names of
the Board of Directors, $8.00 - $10.00.

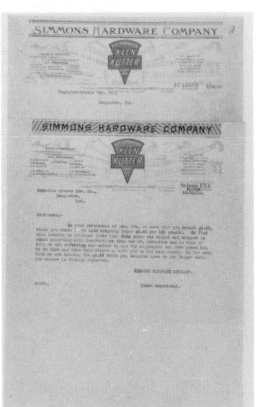

Left Photo:
Letterhead,
two different types from
Simmons Hardware
Company. These were
used in 1911 and 1913,
$8.00 - $10.00 each.

Right Photo:
Letterhead,
Shapleigh Hardware
Company - unused,
$5.00 - $6.00.

Left Photo:
Envelopes,
Winchester-Simmons
Company. Inside of the
envelope are invoices dated
1926 and 1927.
$8.00 - $10.00 each with
invoice.

Right Photo:
Winchester-Simmons
Company envelope and
statement dated 1929,
$8.00 - $10.00 set.

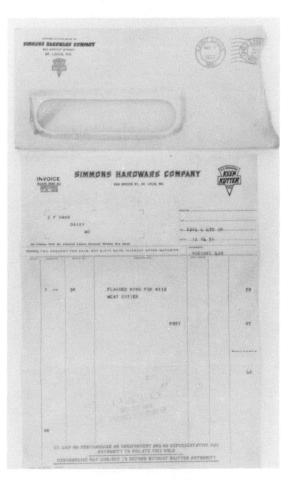

Left Photo:
Invoice with window
envelope dated 1931/1932,
$8.00 - $10.00.

Right Photo:
Envelopes, small, used,
window type, each containing invoice. The back of
these envelopes are very
artistic with tools, razors,
scissors, etc. pictured for
advertisement.
$10.00 - $15.00 each.

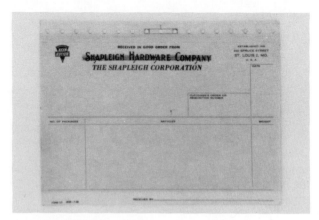

Packing Slip, unused, Shapleigh Corporation,
$7.00 - $8.00.

Freight or Shipping Labels,
$7.00 - $8.00 each.

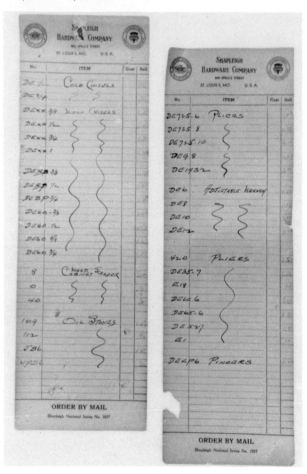

Mail Order paper items, $7.00 - $10.00 each.

Shipping Tape, roll, $25.00 - $30.00.

Shipping Labels, two different styles, back side contains
lines for placement of address,
$7.00 - $8.00 each.

Magazine Advertisement "The Dog Doesn't Mind, He Knows It Won't Hurt - It's A Keen Kutter," $45.00 - $65.00. There is also a postcard out of this same version and it is valued at $65.00 - $85.00.

Magazine Advertisement from the Saturday Evening Post edition of May 5, 1909, $10.00 - $15.00.

Advertisement from a July 17, 1909 Saturday Evening Post, man using workbench tools, $10.00 - $15.00.

Left Photo:
Advertisements ran in magazines. Very artistic the way the circle and emblem were made using small Keen Kutter emblems, $5.00 - $6.00 each.

Right Photo:
Advertisements ran in a 1912 magazine, $5.00 - $6.00 each.

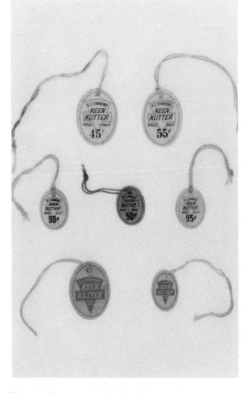

Price Tags, emblem shaped, tie-on type.
Small 1", $2.00 - $3.00 each.
Large 3", $7.00 - $8.00 each.

Price Tags, oval shaped, tie-on type, two-sided, $1.00 - $2.00 each.

Advertisements ran in magazines of tool cabinets, $5.00 - $6.00 each.

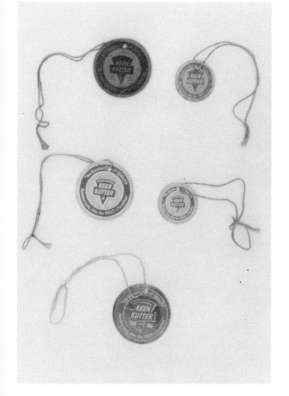

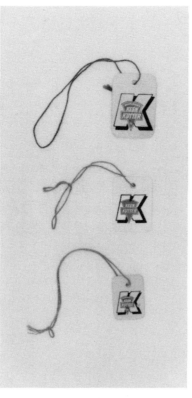

Price Tags, round tie-on type,
$1.00 - $2.00 each.

Price Tags, tie-on type,
Shapleigh, Big K,
75¢ - $1.25 each.

Price Stickers, roll type with gum
back, $20.00 - $25.00 roll.

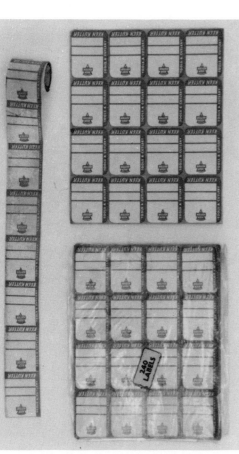

Left Photo:
Labels, packs in sheets, $4.00 - $6.00 per sheet.
Labels, small roll, $4.00 - $6.00.

Bottom Photo:
Hi-Low Bin Tickets #L5448-C for a quick change pricing system on
display racks.   Value of box full, $125.00.

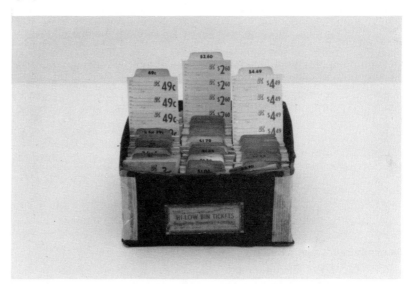

# DISPLAYS

Display Case, 24" deep, 42" high, 72" long, Keen Kutter logos etched in glass, $300.00 - $350.00.

Showcase, 33" base, 33" tall, has curved glass. Etched on the glasses are items it displayed being: Fine Hornet Pocket Knives, Keen Kutter Scissors, Keen Kutter Shears, Keen Kutter Pocket Knives. $600.00.

Bronze Keen Kutter name was mounted on top of the K200 Scissors and Shear Merchandise Case. This case was brought to me complete before I collected Keen Kutter. I bought the name itself, took it off the case, and told the owner to do whatever he wanted to with the case, all I wanted was the name. The case was 29¾" long, 11½" wide and 3½" high at front and 8" high at back with a slant front. I look back now and can't believe I did that! Value of name alone $75.00 - $100.00 (name is 12" long and 1½" high).

Sign: Double sided, yellow sign says Keen Kutter Tools. This is the top of the "Silent Salesman" rack. It is 6" x 59". Value of sign alone, $75.00 - $85.00. Value of "Silent Salesman Rack" $150.00 - $175.00.

Pocket Knife Revolving Display Case, four-sided, 11" x 11" square, 18½" tall.  The top lifts off and any of the four glass panels lift out as do the boards on which the knives are hung.  One photo shows how the case looks with my knives displayed in it.  Case by itself valued $200.00 - $225.00.

Screw driver Display Rack, 24" long, 10½" high, 5½" wide.

The photo on the right shows the manner screw drivers were displayed in the rack. Rack value $100.00 - $125.00.

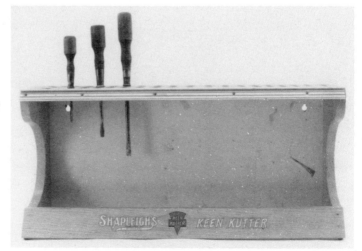

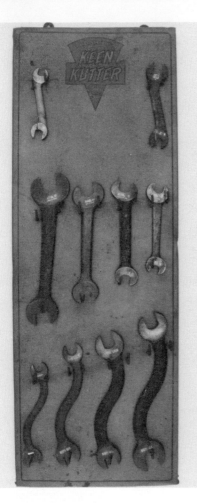

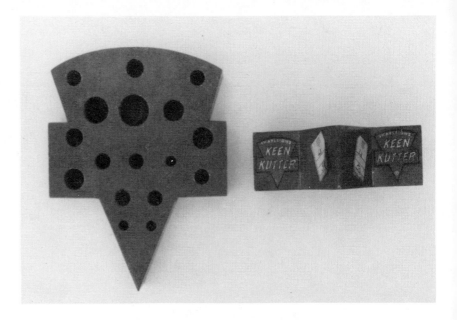

Left Photo: Wrench Assortment Display Board #K30A.
It came with 1 dozen Keen Kutter general purpose and 1½ dozen Keen Kutter textile and machine wrenches. Display board value without wrenches, $150.00 - $200.00.

Top Photo: Chisel and Punch Display Stands, logo design.
Two different sizes. One has 17 holes and is 6" x 8" x 1¾" thick. The other has 24 holes and is 5" x 6½" x 1¾" thick and held nail sets. They are both Shapleigh. $35.00 - $45.00 each.

Left Photo:
Paint Rack #275, color card holder.
Tin case 15¼" high, 11¼" wide, 4¾" deep. Yellow finish with black and red lettering, $150.00 - $175.00.

Top Photo:
Wooden Electric Tool Rack. 31" wide, 28" high, $100.00 - $125.00.

Garden Tool Rack, three shelves, color green. Keen Kutter is embossed on the top front shelf. Legs are made from shovel handles. One photo shows how it looks with tools displayed on it. Rack value $100.00 - $125.00.

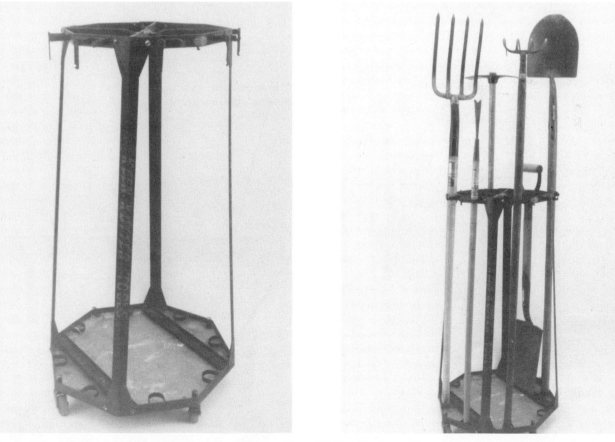

Garden Tool Rack, octagon shaped, color black. Keen Kutter Tools written down the side. This also came in the color yellow. Rack value $100.00 - $125.00.

Garden Tool Rack, metal, $100.00 - $125.00.

Garden Tool Display Rack, metal. Green with orange letters, 4' long, 6" wide, fastens direct to the wall, $75.00 - $95.00.

Paper Holder with 12" roll of paper. Two photos showing front and back view.

Roll of paper by itself, $125.00 - $150.00.
Paper Holder without paper, $75.00 - $100.00.

Paper Holder, double rack.
18" top rack and a 24" bottom rack, contains string,
$175.00 - $200.00.

Knife Display for kitchen knives.
Display without knives $100.00 - $125.00.

This photo shows how knives were displayed.

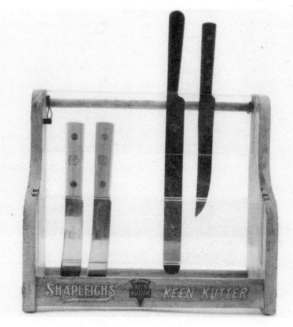

# MISCELLANEOUS

Pocket watch, achievement award. Elgin 21 jewel, 14K solid gold, Dec. 1938. Front and back view shown. Value $750.00 and up.

Puzzle (pictured put together) with its original box. E.C. Simmons, $200.00 - $250.00.

Watch fob for a vest coat, 10KGF Standard of America. Has a salesman's name on back. $75.00 - $100.00.

Lapel Pin shaped like an axe head, $50.00 - $65.00.

Left Photo:
Top: Pin clip-on. Given free at times with a knife purchase, $10.00 - $15.00.
Bottom: Lapel Pin, $25.00 - $30.00.

Fob: this is a reproduction, $10.00. The original one like this, $65.00 - $85.00.

Lapel Pin, stick pin type, shaped like the emblem. This is a reproduction, $5.00 - $6.00.

118

Padlock, E.C. Simmons
Santa Fe Signal Lock. Front
side has the keyhole cover;
back side says Santa Fe.
$300.00 - $350.00.

Padlock, Santa Fe Railroad.
Front side says Keen
Kutter; back side says
Santa Fe.
$300.00 - $350.00.

Padlocks, E.C. Simmons emblem-shaped with plain shackle. One photo shows the front view which has E.C. Simmons written above Keen Kutter. The backs have Keen Kutter written on them. $85.00 - $125.00 each.

Padlock, three different types. E.C. Simmons written on the shackle, and they are shaped like the Keen Kutter emblem. One photo shows the fronts and the other, the back view. The lock on the right (back view) has a smooth back. $85.00 - $125.00 each.

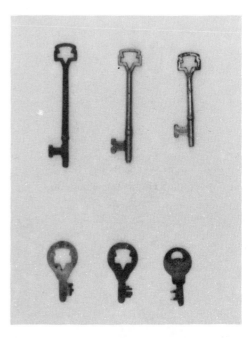

Left Photo:
Trunk Lock, E.C. Simmons, $65.00 - $75.00.

Right Photo:
Skeleton Keys: Keyhole emblem-shaped, $12.00 - $18.00 each. Padlock Keys: The left and middle have the emblem for the keyhole, the other just has # stamped out, $12.00 - $18.00 each.

Wagon, Keen Kutter Jet. Color - red; 15½" x 34", $150.00 - $200.00.

Wagon, Keen Kutter Rocket (Lifetime Bearings). 16½" x 35", light brown metallic, $150.00 - $200.00.

Wagon, Keen Kutter Rocket (ball bearings). 15½" x 34", $150.00 - $200.00.

Wagon, Keen Kutter #98, 15½" x 34",
$150.00 - $200.00.

Wagon, Keen Kutter Supreme, 16½" x 35".
This one is valued at only $75.00 - $100.00
due to its condition.

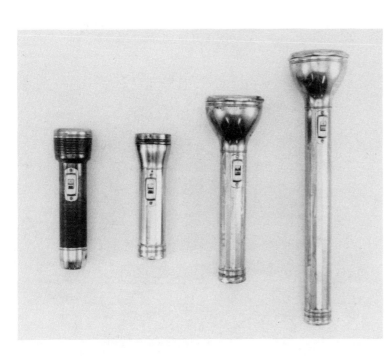

Flashlights: Left one is a two cell; next three are a set
with the same design and octagon shape consisting of
a two cell, three cell and five cell,
$35.00 - $55.00 each.

Flashlight: end view showing the marking.

Left Photo:
Paint Can,
1 quart shellac
container, $40.00.
Paint Brush, 1½"
marked Keen Kutter,
$40.00.

Right Photo:
Painter's Hat,
E.C. Simmons,
store give-away for
purchasing paint,
$35.00 - $40.00.

Left: Cast iron emblem, original, $15.00 - $20.00.
Right: Brass emblem, possible reproduction, $25.00.

Holster, leather for gun.  Emblem is in
the lower left corner, $45.00.

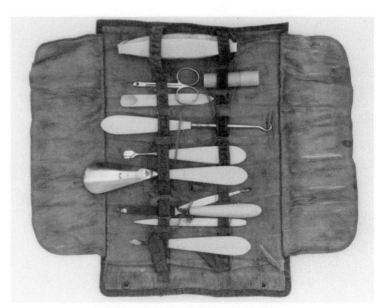

Manicure Set.  The scissors, shoe horn and nail file
are marked with the Keen Kutter emblem.  The set
has celluloid ivory handles.  $60.00 - $70.00.

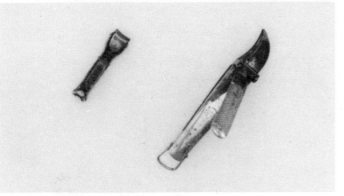

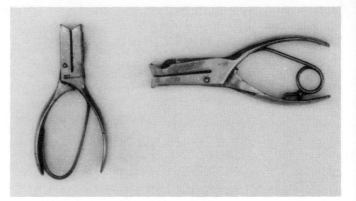

Nail Clipper, patent August 16, 1910, $35.00.
Toe Nail Clipper, $35.00.

Hole Punches, two different styles, used for paper, $25.00 - $35.00 each.

Left Photo:
Minnow Bucket, Shapleigh, $100.00 - $125.00.

Right Photo:
Spool of Fishing String, Shapleigh, $15.00 - $20.00 in this condition. Mint condition, $35.00 - $45.00.

# ELECTRICAL TOOLS

Electric Power Saw, 7" Model KK70, $40.00 - $50.00.

Clutch Saw, 7" Model KK258GK, $40.00 - $50.00.

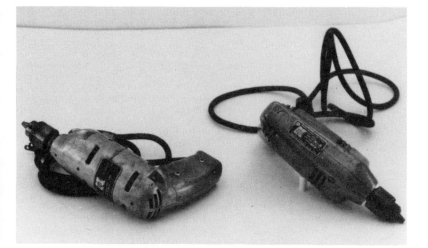

Jig Saw, Shapleigh Model KK249, $30.00 - $40.00.

Drill, ¼" Shapleigh Model KK243B, $25.00 - $30.00.
Drill, ¼" Shapleigh Model KK100, $25.00 - $30.00.

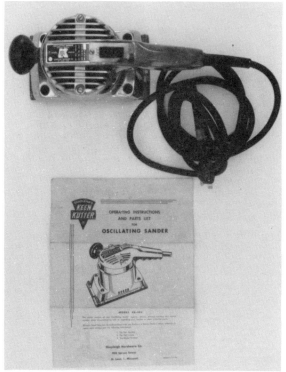

Hedge Trimmer, Shapleigh Model KK57, $30.00 - $40.00.

Oscillating Sander Model KK242 with operating instructions and parts list, $50.00 - $65.00.

Bench Grinder, 4½" Shapleigh, electric,
$40.00 - $50.00.

Rip Saw Blade, 8" in original carton. Blade is mint, Shapleigh,
$30.00 - $40.00.

Rip Saw Blade, 5½" in original carton. Blade
is mint, Shapleigh, $30.00 - $40.00.

Circular Saw Blade, 8" Val-Test Corp.,
Chicago, IL, $8.00 - $10.00.

# Books on Antiques and Collectibles

Most of the following books are available from your local book seller or antique dealer, or on loan from your public library. If you are unable to locate certain titles in your area you may order by mail from COLLECTOR BOOKS, P.O. Box 3009, Paducah, KY 42002-3009. Add $2.00 for postage for the first book ordered and $.25 for each additional book. Include item number, title and price when ordering. Allow 14 to 21 days for delivery. All books are well illustrated and contain current values.

## Books on Glass and Pottery

| | | |
|---|---|---|
| 1810 | American Art Glass, Shuman | $29.95 |
| 1517 | American Belleek, Gaston | $19.95 |
| 2016 | Bedroom & Bathroom Glassware of the Depression Years | $19.95 |
| 1312 | Blue & White Stoneware, McNerney | $9.95 |
| 1959 | Blue Willow, 2nd Ed., Gaston | $14.95 |
| 1627 | Children's Glass Dishes, China & Furniture II, Lechler | $19.95 |
| 1892 | Collecting Royal Haeger, Garmon | $19.95 |
| 2017 | Collector's Ency. of Depression Glass, Florence, 9th Ed. | $19.95 |
| 1373 | Collector's Ency of Amercian Dinnerware, Cunningham | $24.95 |
| 1812 | Collector's Ency. of Fiesta, Huxford | $19.95 |
| 1439 | Collector's Ency. of Flow Blue China, Gaston | $19.95 |
| 1961 | Collector's Ency of Fry Glass, Fry Glass Society | $24.95 |
| 1813 | Collector's Encyclopedia of Geisha Girl Porcelain, Litts | $19.95 |
| 1664 | Collector's Ency. of Heisey Glass, Bredehoft | $24.95 |
| 1915 | Collector's Ency. of Hall China, 2nd Ed., Whitmyer | $19.95 |
| 1358 | Collector's Ency. of McCoy Pottery, Huxford | $19.95 |
| 1039 | Collector's Ency. of Nippon Porcelain I, Van Patten | $19.95 |
| 1350 | Collector's Ency. of Nippon Porcelain II, Van Patten | $19.95 |
| 1665 | Collector's Ency. of Nippon Porcelain III, Van Patten | $24.95 |
| 1447 | Collector's Ency. of Noritake, Van Patten | $19.95 |
| 1038 | Collector's Ency. of Occupied Japan, 2nd Ed., Florence | $14.95 |
| 1719 | Collector's Ency. of Occupied Japan III, Florence | $19.95 |
| 2019 | Collector's Ency. of Occupied Japan IV, Florence | $14.95 |
| 1715 | Collector's Ency. of R.S. Prussia II, Gaston | $24.95 |
| 1034 | Collector's Ency. of Roseville Pottery, Huxford | $19.95 |
| 1035 | Collector's Ency. of Roseville Pottery, 2nd Ed., Huxford | $19.95 |
| 1623 | Coll. Guide to Country Stoneware & Pottery, Raycraft | $9.95 |
| 1523 | Colors in Cambridge, National Cambridge Society | $19.95 |
| 1425 | Cookie Jars, Westfall | $9.95 |
| 1843 | Covered Animal Dishes, Grist | $14.95 |
| 1844 | Elegant Glassware of the Depression Era, 3rd Ed., Florence | $19.95 |
| 2024 | Kitchen Glassware of the Depression Years, 4th Florence | $19.95 |
| 1465 | Haviland Collectibles & Art Objects, Gaston | $19.95 |
| 1917 | Head Vases Id & Value Guide, Cole | $14.95 |
| 1392 | Majolica Pottery, Katz-Marks | $9.95 |
| 1669 | Majolica Pottery, 2nd Series, Katz-Marks | $9.95 |
| 1919 | Pocket Guide to Depression Glass, 6th Ed., Florence | $9.95 |
| 1438 | Oil Lamps II, Thuro | $19.95 |
| 1670 | Red Wing Collectibles, DePasquale | $9.95 |
| 1440 | Red Wing Stoneware, DePasquale | $9.95 |
| 1958 | So. Potteries Blue Ridge Dinnerware, 3rd Ed., Newbound | $14.95 |
| 1889 | Standard Carnival Glass, 2nd Ed., Edwards | $24.95 |
| 1941 | Standard Carnival Glass Price Guide, Edwards | $7.95 |
| 1814 | Wave Crest, Glass of C.F. Monroe, Cohen | $29.95 |
| 1848 | Very Rare Glassware of the Depression Years, Florence | $24.95 |

## Books on Dolls & Toys

| | | |
|---|---|---|
| 1887 | American Rag Dolls, Patino | $14.95 |
| 1749 | Black Dolls, Gibbs | $14.95 |
| 1514 | Character Toys & Collectibles 1st Series, Longest | $19.95 |
| 1750 | Character Toys & Collectibles, 2nd Series, Longest | $19.95 |
| 2021 | Collectible Male Action Figures, Manos | $14.95 |
| 1529 | Collector's Ency. of Barbie Dolls, DeWein | $19.95 |
| 1066 | Collector's Ency. of Half Dolls, Marion | $29.95 |
| 1891 | French Dolls in Color, 3rd Series, Smith | $14.95 |
| 1631 | German Dolls, Smith | $9.95 |
| 1635 | Horsman Dolls, Gibbs | $19.95 |
| 1067 | Madame Alexander Collector's Dolls, Smith | $19.95 |
| 2025 | Madame Alexander Price Guide #15, Smith | $7.95 |
| 1995 | Modern Collectors Dolls, Vol. I, Smith | $19.95 |

| | | |
|---|---|---|
| 1516 | Modern Collector's Dolls V, Smith | $19.95 |
| 1540 | Modern Toys, 1930-1980, Baker | $19.95 |
| 2033 | Patricia Smith Doll Values, Antique to Modern, 6th ed., | $9.95 |
| 1886 | Stern's Guide to Disney | $14.95 |
| 1513 | Teddy Bears & Steiff Animals, Mandel | $9.95 |
| 1817 | Teddy Bears & Steiff Animals, 2nd, Mandel | $19.95 |
| 2028 | Toys, Antique & Collectible, Longest | $14.95 |
| 1630 | Vogue, Ginny Dolls, Smith | $19.95 |
| 1648 | World of Alexander-Kins, Smith | $19.95 |
| 1808 | Wonder of Barbie, Manos | $9.95 |
| 1430 | World of Barbie Dolls, Manos | $9.95 |

## Other Collectibles

| | | |
|---|---|---|
| 1457 | American Oak Furniture, McNerney | $9.95 |
| 1846 | Antique & Collectible Marbles, Grist, 2nd Ed. | $9.95 |
| 1712 | Antique & Collectible Thimbles, Mathis | $19.95 |
| 1880 | Antique Iron, McNerney | $9.95 |
| 1748 | Antique Purses, Holiner | $19.95 |
| 1868 | Antique Tools, Our American Heritage, McNerney | $9.95 |
| 2015 | Archaic Indian Points & Knives, Edler | $14.95 |
| 1426 | Arrowheads & Projectile Points, Hothem | $7.95 |
| 1278 | Art Nouveau & Art Deco Jewelry, Baker | $9.95 |
| 1714 | Black Collectibles, Gibbs | $19.95 |
| 1666 | Book of Country, Raycraft | $19.95 |
| 1960 | Book of Country Vol II, Raycraft | $19.95 |
| 1811 | Book of Moxie, Potter | $29.95 |
| 1128 | Bottle Pricing Guide, 3rd Ed., Cleveland | $7.95 |
| 1751 | Christmas Collectibles, Whitmyer | $19.95 |
| 1752 | Christmas Ornaments, Johnston | $19.95 |
| 1713 | Collecting Barber Bottles, Holiner | $24.95 |
| 2018 | Collector's Ency. of Graniteware, Greguire | $24.95 |
| 1634 | Coll. Ency. of Salt & Pepper Shakers, Davern | $19.95 |
| 2020 | Collector's Ency. of Salt & Pepper Shakers II, Davern | $19.95 |
| 1916 | Collector's Guide to Art Deco, Gaston | $14.95 |
| 1753 | Collector's Guide to Baseball Memorabilia, Raycraft | $14.95 |
| 1537 | Collector's Guide to Country Baskets, Raycraft | $9.95 |
| 1437 | Collector's Guide to Country Furniture, Raycraft | $9.95 |
| 1842 | Collector's Guide to Country Furniture II, Raycraft | $14.95 |
| 1962 | Collector's Guide to Decoys, Huxford | $14.95 |
| 1441 | Collector's Guide to Post Cards, Wood | $9.95 |
| 1716 | Fifty Years of Fashion Jewelry, Baker | $19.95 |
| 2022 | Flea Market Trader, 6th Ed., Huxford | $9.95 |
| 1668 | Flint Blades & Proj. Points of the No. Am. Indian, Tully | $24.95 |
| 1755 | Furniture of the Depression Era, Swedberg | $19.95 |
| 1424 | Hatpins & Hatpin Holders, Baker | $9.95 |
| 1964 | Indian Axes & Related Stone Artifacts, Hothem | $14.95 |
| 2023 | Keen Kutter Collectibles, 2nd Ed., Heuring | $14.95 |
| 1212 | Marketplace Guide to Oak Furniture, Blundell | $17.95 |
| 1918 | Modern Guns, Id. & Values, 7th Ed., Quertermous | $12.95 |
| 1181 | 100 Years of Collectible Jewelry, Baker | $9.95 |
| 1965 | Pine Furniture, Our Am. Heritage, McNerney | $14.95 |
| 1124 | Primitives, Our American Heritage, McNerney | $8.95 |
| 1759 | Primitives, Our American Heritage, 2nd Series, McNerney | $14.95 |
| 2026 | Railroad Collectibles, 4th Ed., Baker | $14.95 |
| 1632 | Salt & Pepper Shakers, Guarnaccia | $9.95 |
| 1888 | Salt & Pepper Shakers II, Guarnaccia | $14.95 |
| 1816 | Silverplated Flatware, 3rd Ed., Hagan | $14.95 |
| 2027 | Standard Baseball Card Pr. Gd., Florence | $9.95 |
| 1922 | Standard Bottle Pr. Gd., Sellari | $14.95 |
| 1966 | Standard Fine Art Value Guide, Huxford | $29.95 |
| 1890 | The Old Book Value Guide | $19.95 |
| 1923 | Wanted to Buy | $9.95 |
| 1885 | Victorian Furniture, McNerney | $9.95 |

# Schroeder's Antiques Price Guide

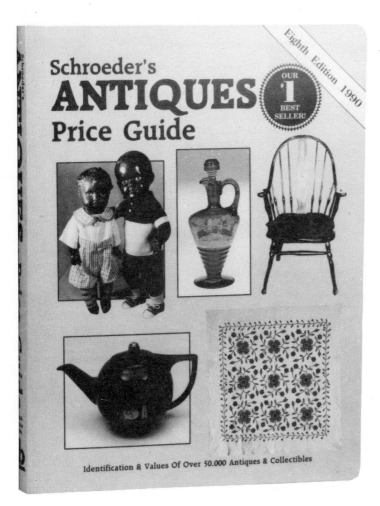

*Schroeder's Antiques Price Guide* has climbed its way to the top in a field already supplied with several well-established publications! The word is out, *Schroeder's Price Guide* is the best buy at any price. Over 500 categories are covered, with more than 50,000 listings. But it's not volume alone that makes Schroeder's the unique guide it is recognized to be. From ABC Plates to Zsolnay, if it merits the interest of today's collector, you'll find it in Schroeder's. Each subject is represented with histories and background information. In addition, hundreds of sharp original photos are used each year to illustrate not only the rare and the unusual, but the everyday "fun-type" collectibles as well -- not postage stamp pictures, but large close-up shots that show important details clearly.

Each edition is completely re-typeset from all new sources. We have not and will not simply change prices in each new edition. All new copy and all new illustrations make Schroeder's THE price guide on antiques and collectibles.

The writing and researching team behind this giant is proportionately large. It is backed by a staff of more than seventy of Collector Books' finest authors, as well as a board of advisors made up of well-known antique authorities and the country's top dealers, all specialists in their fields. Accuracy is their primary aim. Prices are gathered over the entire year previous to publication, from ads and personal contacts. Then each category is thoroughly checked to spot inconsistencies, listings that may not be entirely reflective of actual market dealings, and lines too vague to be of merit.

Only the best of the lot remains for publication. You'll find *Schroeder's Antiques Price Guide* the one to buy for factual information and quality.

No dealer, collector or investor can afford not to own this book. It is available from your favorite bookseller or antiques dealer at the low price of $12.95. If you are unable to find this price guide in your area, it's available from Collector Books, P. O. Box 3009, Paducah, KY 42001 at $12.95 plus $2.00 for postage and handling.

8½ x 11, 608 Pages                                                                                       $12.95

**COLLECTOR BOOKS**
*A Division of Schroeder Publishing Co., Inc.*